PROTECT
· YOUR ·
Lifestyle

Make Empowered, Educated,
and Effective Personal Insurance Decisions

MEAGHAN DOWD

Personal Risk Advisor

Protect Your Lifestyle

Make Empowered, Educated, and Effective Personal Insurance Decisions

Meaghan Dowd

Published by WENK Publishing, Saint Louis, MO

Project Management and Book Design: Davis Creative, LLC / CreativePublishingPartners.com

Publisher's Cataloging-in-Publication

(Provided by Cassidy Cataloguing Services, Inc.).

Names:	Dowd, Meaghan, author.
Title:	Protect your lifestyle : make empowered, educated, and effective personal insurance decisions / Meaghan Dowd, Personal Risk Advisor.
Description:	Saint Louis, MO : WENK Publishing, [2024]
Identifiers:	ISBN: 979-8-9897008-0-6 (paperback) | 979-8-9897008-1-3 (ebook) | LCCN: 2023922656
Subjects:	LCSH: Property insurance. | Casualty insurance. | Finance, Personal. | Wealth. | Financial risk management. | BISAC: BUSINESS & ECONOMICS / Insurance / General. | BUSINESS & ECONOMICS / Finance / Wealth Management. | BUSINESS & ECONOMICS / Finance / Financial Risk Management.
Classification:	LCC: HG8051 .D68 2024 | DDC: 368.1--dc23

ATTENTION CORPORATIONS, UNIVERSITIES, COLLEGES AND PROFESSIONAL ORGANIZATIONS: Quantity discounts are available on bulk purchases of this book for educational, gift purposes, or as premiums for increasing magazine subscriptions or renewals. Special books or book excerpts can also be created to fit specific needs. For information, please contact Meaghan Dowd, WENK Publishing, wenkllc23@gmail.com, and https://wenkpublishing.com.

DISCLAIMER: This book is intended as a general introduction and overview of the issues related to auto, home, valuables, and excess liability insurance. The author is neither an attorney nor a CPA, and insurance requirements and regulations vary widely across the country and by company. All insurance-related decisions should be made in consultation with the appropriate qualified advisors under your specific circumstances, and the reader should not rely solely on the contents of this book in making insurance decisions.

Table of Contents

Preface

Everyone I meet has a vision for their life. Some people pursue deep passions and big dreams. Others prioritize spending time with family and enjoying life's simple pleasures. Everyone's lifestyle is unique. We live in a crazy, often unpredictable world and in a litigious society. Life happens. It might find you at the wrong place at the wrong time, a victim of an unfortunate accident. Are you prepared if you experience a loss?

I hope you picked up this book because you want to learn about protecting your lifestyle. Or maybe you're wondering whether the information in this book applies to you or your clients. Or perhaps you'd like to learn about considerations related to your personal insurance.

If you're unsure whether you're exposed or prepared, read this book then talk with a risk advisor.

What's a risk advisor? A risk advisor is an individual who reviews your everyday activities: the distance you drive to work, your home and its contents, the advisory boards you sit on, what you do for fun, and how you title your home and autos. They take a 360-degree view of your life to assess what could go wrong, how it could go wrong, and how to protect your assets.

Why do YOU need a risk advisor? You work extremely hard for everything you have, and if one day that was left vulnerable due to a bad car accident or loss in a fire, what would you do?

A risk advisor can help plan for these situations before they occur and provide solutions to protect you, your family, and your most valuable assets.

Something to note is that most risk advisors hold property and casualty insurance licenses like an insurance agent. The difference between the two is how they use their license. Insurance agents are usually looking to sell a product, regardless of whether the product provides a solution to your needs. A risk advisor is someone who looks at your life and the actual needs that arise and finds the right solutions based on your needs, risk tolerance, and expectation at time of claim. These terms are sometimes used interchangeably, but it is important to understand the difference and choose the best personal insurance partner for you.

MEET THE AUTHOR

I am Meaghan Dowd. I'm so pleased you found this book because I know it will help you, and I love helping people protect their lifestyle!

Coming from a family of attorneys, I've seen a wide range of scenarios where insurance was the make-it-or-break-it piece of the discussion. I've seen what can happen due to improper insurance coverage and witnessed firsthand families lose businesses and earnings. I've also seen insurance help individuals, families, and businesses to overcome an accident and not lose it all because of one bad day. My mission in writing this book is to help people feel empowered about their insurance decisions and save others from that unnecessary heartache and loss due to improper insurance coverage.

During my career helping people learn about and understand insurance, I have become extremely passionate about insurance! Insurance creates peace of mind. It allows you to plan for worst-case scenarios and to protect yourself, so if the worst-case scenario does occur, you know you have the right protection in place and can continue living the life you have built with little change.

> **"The difference between an insurance advisor (like Meaghan) and a typical insurance agent is like the difference between a master chef and a short-order cook. You're going to get fed by both...but one has the skill and resources that the other simply can't provide."**
>
> *– R. M., Financial Advisor*

WHAT IS LIFESTYLE PROTECTION?

It depends on the person. Whether it's traveling the world, sailing the Caribbean, running or starting a business, joining a board, collecting art or cars, or starting a family, everyone lives life in their own way.

Most people do not think about the hidden exposures that come along with everyday life. That's okay—why would you? This book isn't to deter you from living life whatsoever! It's a how-to guide to living life while protecting everything you love and for which you've labored.

Chapter 1:

Insurance Basics

What is insurance? In short, insurance is simply the transfer of risk from one person to another or to a company. In personal insurance, this has two forms: Property (homes, valuables, vehicles) and Liability. This chapter will explain some of the industry jargon and hidden risks you may not be aware of, so you'll have some base knowledge going into the rest of this book.

LOSING LIFE OPPORTUNITIES

How would the opportunities that you have for spending time with friends, family, vacations, and hobbies be impacted if you are not fully protected?

Unfortunately, suffering a loss that is not fully protected can force people to take actions such as digging into their savings or 401(k) with the penalties for early withdrawal, getting a second job, moving in with their in-laws, deferring retirement, or draining their investments. The possibilities are endless and rarely desirable.

Take the time to read this book, understand your hidden exposures, and find a risk advisor you trust to help protect you.

TRANSFER OF RISK – PROPERTY

Example: You purchase a new home, securing your dream kitchen, master bath, man cave, and beautifully landscaped yard. Your family has been settled in for a few years, and then one stormy night as you sleep tight, a lightning bolt hits your home!

You rush to round up your family and get out. Calling 911, you might be thinking, "What's next?" Hopefully, you have family or friends in the area where you can stay for the night and strategize.

Eventually these questions will run through your mind: "How am I going to rebuild my home? All our property is destroyed, and we need a place to stay, but we still have to pay the mortgage and can't afford two home payments."

Great news: With the right insurance, these worries would be addressed! You would only have to worry about your deductible (if that). You would transfer the cost of rebuilding your home, personal property replacement, additional living cost, and more to the insurance company through the **transfer of risk**.

DEDUCTIBLE

The **deductible** is the portion of the loss you are responsible for at the time a covered claim occurs.

In the previous example, let's say at the time you chose your homeowners policy, you opted for a $2,500 deductible and your home replacement cost is $650,000. After the fire occurred, you would only have to pay $2,500 and would have your home rebuilt, personal property replaced, and additional cost of living covered.

How amazing does that sound? Not a bad trade-off!

Side note: With certain insurance companies, you could have your deductible waived if the claim is over a certain dollar amount (typically around $50,000 in damages).

With auto insurance, there are two different deductibles: comprehensive deductible and collision deductible. These will both apply to damage done to your vehicle. We usually see around $1,000 to $5,000 for these auto deductibles, and we'll talk about the difference in the Auto Insurance chapter.

Choosing the Wrong Deductible

Consider this when choosing your deductible: The insurance company is like a bank. When you file a claim, you "borrow" money from them that includes "interest," also known as a surcharge, over a 3- to 5-year period.

You want to avoid filing small claims and reserve insurance for the financially devastating losses that you cannot afford out of pocket. While the $6,000 burst pipe is not an ideal expense, if you have the funds available, it is cheaper to pay out of pocket than to use insurance. If it's a $60,000 burst pipe, that is where you'd want to use insurance.

TRANSFER OF RISK – LIABILITY

Example: You have friends over to your house, and while the kids are having a great time on the playset, one kid falls off and is severely injured. The child is in the hospital for a few weeks, undergoes physical therapy for 2 years, and will have permanent damage to a leg that will limit future activity.

Your guest can come after you for the incurred cost of the child's medical bills and change in lifestyle for the child's future. Maybe one of the parents will need to take a leave of absence from work to take care of the child. The costs associated with this type of loss can add up quickly. And that is why liability losses are so scary because you never know who is going to get hurt and how badly.

Choosing the Wrong Liability Limit

When choosing the right liability limit, think about your current assets and net worth as well as future income and assets.

Consider what you do every day: Are you just commuting to and from work? Or are you often hosting friends in your home? Maybe you drive around all weekend for sports or travel for fun?

The more you do, the greater the chance of a loss occurring. The activities you engage in will determine the severity of potential losses. Choosing the wrong liability limit allows an injured party to go through the courts to pursue your personal assets to make them whole again once they have exhausted your insurance limits.

Personal assets include cash, the equity in your home, money in the market— or worse, you might be forced to liquidate assets or have your wages or salary garnished.

You may be thinking there must be a high cost associated with this kind of coverage. Truth is, the cost is less than you spend on your daily coffee.

When discussing wealth, most people focus on making a lot of money— the offensive approach. Few take the time to consider the defensive side of wealth-building, which is risk management. Throughout this book, we will explore how your lifestyle directs your risk exposure and clearly outline the types of hidden risks you face and the protection available.

Chapter 2:
Homeowners Insurance

Your home is yours. Just like you, it is unique. Each aspect of your home and lifestyle should be considered when looking at homeowners coverage. Whether you own or rent, there is a reason you said yes! And those are the details that will matter at the time of rebuilding your life after a loss occurs.

Close your eyes. Remember when you were house hunting and looking at different properties? What specifically called you to this home? Was it the custom chef's kitchen? The finished basement? The outdoor oasis? Maybe you had a vision and invested into making that a reality. Or perhaps the school district or proximity to your favorite amenities were factors? No detail is too small.

Throughout this chapter, we are going to break down your home and different risks to consider when crafting your personal home insurance program.

THE BASICS: POLICY FORMS

Most people have heard of a declarations page and swear by it as a way to understand their insurance coverage. However, the declarations page is just a snapshot and sometimes doesn't accurately represent what is actually covered, let alone how it is being covered. The declarations lay out the specific dollar amounts that the insurance company could potentially be responsible for. I use the word *potentially* because it is the actual policy form the homeowner chooses at time of purchase that dictates what losses are covered and how they are covered. The 90-plus pages of insurance jargon behind the declaration are what really matter when purchasing and reviewing your insurance coverage.

Allow me to demystify the eight common types of homeowners' forms available for purchase. Usually, your advisor will choose the type of homeowners' form, but it's important to understand the differences as the form determines which losses are covered and how they are covered.

Note: The breakdowns below are general descriptions of each form. Every insurance company can file its own forms and adjustments, but most use the Insurance Services Office (ISO) forms as the basis for their products. It's important to read your specific policy for details pertaining to your coverage.

HO-1 – Basic Form: We rarely see these anymore, but this is the most basic of insurance policies covering only your home on an actual cash value basis with *NO* other structures, personal property, or liability coverages. The typical losses we see covered are fire or lightning; windstorm or hail; riot or civil commotion; damage from aircraft, vehicles, smoke, malicious mischief, or vandalism; and volcanic eruption.

HO-2 – Broad Form: Still uncommon in the marketplace, this policy covers your home on a replacement cost basis as well as other structures, but personal property is covered on actual cash value. Clients also can include liability and medical payments on this form. The losses covered are the same as HO-1 plus a few others such as falling objects, sleet, freezing conditions, or weight of ice and snow.

HO-3 – Special Form: This is one of the more common ones for insuring a primary home. The coverage for the dwelling itself is the actual cost of rebuilding, referred to sometimes as replacement coverage, and the losses covered broaden to cover direct physical loss to dwelling and other structures except for those specifically excluded in the policy, which is known as "open perils" coverage. Some common exclusions are flood, earthquake, landslide, and sinkhole. These can be added for an additional cost (also known as endorsed) onto some policies depending on the insurance company. The personal property, however, is still covered on a named peril basis, so only losses listed in the policy will be covered.

HO-4 – Renters, aka tenant's, insurance: This type of policy is used for renters (the individual who will be living in the space, not the person leasing the space), as it does not provide dwelling protection and only provides coverage for personal property on an actual cash value basis, loss of use, and personal liability for the renter as the tenant. Renters policies do have endorsements available such as replacement cost for personal property, water backup, and other coverages that may be necessary to better protect your lifestyle.

- HO-14 is a new ISO form as of March 2022 that automatically includes replacement cost of personal property as well as potential allowances for additional endorsements like home sharing and bed bugs.

- If you are renting or just living with someone where you do not have financial interest in the home and are not related to that person, always purchase renters insurance. It is very affordable and provides basic coverage to keep your life afloat should you experience a covered loss.

HO-5 – Comprehensive Form: This is the broadest form of homeowners coverage, and it includes open perils coverage for the dwelling, other structures, and personal property. This means the insured has coverage for direct physical loss unless specifically excluded. This puts the onus back on the insurance company to prove where in the policy language the loss is excluded and thus there is no coverage, meaning you will be paying for the damages out of pocket. Always purchase this form when available.

In some states such as North Carolina, this is the HE form, which can be enhanced further to the HE-7 w/HE20 or HE-7 w/HE21. These enhancements can include coverages like mortgage expense coverage, higher special limits, and enhanced other coverages.

HO-6: This type of policy is for condo owners, and it covers the walls of the structure as the exterior is covered by the master policy. It is important to read the condo association's bylaws to confirm how much coverage is necessary for your unit.

- Townhomes or row homes can be tricky as they could fall into different policy forms based on the association bylaws. Some will require exterior and interior coverage, which would commonly be on HO-3 or HO-5. In other instances, they may only require "walls in" coverage, in which case the HO-6 form is appropriate.

- I can't emphasize this enough: READ THE BYLAWS and send the bylaws to your insurance advisor to make sure you have the required coverage!

HO-7: This policy is used to protect mobile and manufactured homes along with personal property on a named peril basis. The age, size, and build of the home does affect the cost and eligibility with certain companies.

HO-8: This form is commonly used for older homes where the replacement cost exceeds the client's investment or market value. It is a named perils policy, which typically covers about 10 types of losses and covers the structures on an actual cash value basis, which takes into account depreciation at time of a loss.

There is "last resort coverage," aka Fair Plan coverage, which varies from state to state. Clients find themselves looking to the Fair Plan for homes that are ineligible in the standard markets due to the risk profile. This could be loss history at the location or the area and its exposure to catastrophes. Whatever the case, ONLY consider this once all other options are exhausted (even if that means finding a new advisor to provide the right solution).

THE BASICS: YOUR DECLARATIONS PAGE

Dwelling Limit: This coverage protects the structure of your home. The limit you see on the dwelling line of a declaration determines the amount of money you have available from the insurance company to rebuild your home and how your home is going to be rebuilt at the time of loss. You should *always* carry replacement cost coverage when insuring your home. As we already discussed, there are two common types of coverages: actual cash value or replacement cost.

- **Actual Cash Value:** The true value of the home at time of loss, which takes into consideration the normal wear and tear with depreciation of the item(s).

  Example: You have a small kitchen fire, and there is damage to the stove, a few cabinets, and some flooring. The cost to repair and replace the damage is $20,000; however, the kitchen was last updated 10 years ago, and you have actual cash value coverage. The insurance company is only going to pay you a portion of the $20,000 based on the condition of those items. For simplicity, let's say the floor, cabinets, and stove had been used for about 50% of their life expectancy, the insurance company will pay you $10,000 (minus the deductible).

- **Replacement Cost:** The amount the insurance company will pay to replace your home and make you whole again up to the dwelling limit. The replacement cost is calculated based on the specific features and quality of your home. No feature is too small to discuss with your advisor when coming up with this cost.

  - **Hidden Risk:** Your roof material matters! We've seen roofs become a major concern in underwriting with companies over the last decade. The age and material play major factors in the cost and eligibility of a home. Insurance companies cover roofs in a variety of ways. Some offer replacement cost, while others opt for actual cash value or a sliding-scale value or partial replacement where only the damaged shingle is replaced (even if that means the shingles on your roof do not match). It is important to understand this part of a policy when reviewing coverages.

    Example: Your home's roof is 22 years old and the expected life per the shingle company is 30 years. You originally paid $27,500 for it. If your homeowners policy has a clause that changes the language on roof damage to actual cash value or payment scale, you will foot most of that bill if damage occurs. Essentially, the insurance company will cover only the cost for the remaining life of the roof. In other words, the roof has "used up" 75% of its life. You will get $6,875, which is 25% of the total cost.

  - **Hidden Risk:** Have your major systems been updated? Many insurance companies assume as part of the insurance contract that your HVAC, electric, and plumbing systems are up-to-date and in good working order. However, some exclusions apply for certain types of wiring like knob and tube or galvanized piping. Make sure you disclose what is behind the walls and review the application for accuracy before signing as that could determine if coverage is available when a loss occurs.

Other Structures: This coverage applies to features such as outbuildings, detached patios, decks, pools, hardscape, driveways, and more. The more extensive your outdoor living, the more this limit needs to be considered. Typically, this limit is 10% to 20% of your dwelling coverage but can be adjusted for a minimal cost to properly cover your outdoor oasis.

Personal Property: If you take your home and dump it upside down, everything that would fall out should be considered in this limit. Your kitchen appliances (if not built in), clothing, toys, electronics, couches, bedroom furnishings, etc. This limit is typically 50% to 75% of your dwelling coverage and, again, should be adjusted to fit your personal needs. There are sub-limits in policies for items such as jewelry, fine art, and other collectibles, so be sure to talk with your advisor about your valued possessions.

There are two main ways insurance companies protect personal property, which can be different from how the dwelling is covered. One is **named peril** (HO-3 form) coverage; the second is **open peril** (HO-5 form) coverage. With named perils, there is a specific list of covered losses, typically fire or lightning; windstorm or hail; explosion; riots; aircraft; vehicles; smoke; vandalism; theft; falling objects; weight of ice, snow, or sleet; accidental discharge or overflow of water or steam; freezing earth movement, mudflow, or volcanic eruption. With open peril coverage, *everything* is covered unless specifically excluded. Some of these coverages can be added back to the policy for an additional premium through an endorsement.

When thinking about your personal property coverage limit, it is important to take these factors into account:

- Where is the property stored? If it's off premises, confirm the amount of coverage you have within your homeowners policy and ascertain whether there are any coverage limits.

- If you have valuable jewelry, an art collection, wine, collectible action figures, or other items of significant value, you will want to consider a valuable article policy also known as "inland marine" coverage to ensure you have full coverage for those specific items. This is an endorsement, aka a rider, on the homeowners policy or can be purchased as an individual policy.

Take inventory of personal property, either with photos or video, and store them on an online cloud backup service and send copies to your advisor for their files. At time of loss, you will be required to show proof of ownership in order for the companies to provide coverage and pay for the loss.

Loss of Use: These funds will help you pay for a temporary home while your home is being rebuilt after a covered loss. The loss of use limit is a key consideration because these funds will determine whether you can stay in the same neighborhood, live in the same style of home, and maintain your current lifestyle. This limit can be stated as a dollar amount limit, number of days limit, or actual loss sustained, meaning they will pay whatever is necessary until your home is ready. Ideally, purchasing the actual loss sustained coverage with no other limitations is the best option for this coverage.

> **Hidden Risk:** There are a million reasons why repairs and rebuilds take longer than expected. While most claims go smoothly, what happens if there is a delay in the supply chain or a labor shortage? Or maybe the loss was a natural catastrophe and multiple homes in the area are damaged. Being able to maintain your lifestyle and move on with life is important. If this coverage is limited, you could run out of coverage before your home is ready and then need to address where you will live the rest of the time.

Liability: Liability coverage protects you and your net worth should someone be injured or should a loss occur due to negligence on your property. It provides defense cost as well as paying for damages such as medical costs and change in lifestyle to the other party. It can even provide coverage off your premises in certain situations such as damages caused to neighbors; for example, your tree falls on their home, or your bathroom leaks on your downstairs neighbor in a condo. Everyone should consider carrying a minimum of $500,000 of liability coverage whether you're a renter, condo owner, or homeowner. The cost is minimal, and you never know what unforeseen accident can happen.

> **Hidden Exposure:** If you're thinking, "I don't do much or have much to sue for," consider this: In 2022, an individual in Texas was cutting his grass and his lawnmower threw a spark, catching the yard on fire. The fire spread, causing nine total losses to neighboring homes. At the very least, the homeowner may need defense coverage to protect himself and fight off the lawsuits that neighboring homeowners might mount against the grass cutter for alleged negligence. Great news: The liability covers the cost of attorneys typically outside the actual limit of liability. However, if the insured is held responsible for the damages to these homes due to some sort of negligence, then the liability is what would pay out to make the other parties whole again. And once the limit on the declarations is exhausted, the insurance company is done, and any additional damages owed would come from the insured directly.

Medical Payments: This is a no-fault coverage and is for guests (third party) only. It's intended to pay out for smaller injuries that arise on premises so the injured party can move on quickly with reimbursement for medical needs that arise due to the loss. A common example: A visitor falls down your stairs and breaks an arm, accruing small medical bills. The homeowner can file a claim with their homeowners insurance to cover those costs.

The coverage limits available vary from company to company; the coverage can be as low as $500 to upwards of $50,000 or more. Purchase the maximum limit offered by your company.

Jargon Breakdown: Endorsements

An insurance **endorsement** is an addition, amendment, or any other type of change you make to the original terms of your insurance policy. Endorsements can include additional coverage such as extended replacement cost, earthquake, water backup (i.e., sump pump failure), service line, and cyber, and others provide additional coverages specific to your lifestyle. Depending on your insurance company, you should confirm you have these coverages either included in the policy or endorsed on.

ADMITTED VS. NON-ADMITTED INSURANCE COMPANIES

Also, understanding if the insurance company is an admitted insurance company or non-admitted insurance company is important.

An **admitted insurance company** is one that complies with state regulation set by the Department of Insurance. This matters because by complying with the regulations, the insurance company is backed by the state's insurance fund, meaning if the insurance company was to become insolvent (unable to financially pay claims) to policyholders, the state fund would kick in to pay the damages on the insurance company's behalf. The fund does not always guarantee the full rebuild cost, as there are limits that vary by state.

A **non-admitted insurance company** is one that is not regulated by the state, which means they do not qualify for the state's insurance fund, and should the company not be able to pay claims at time of a loss due to financial issues, there is no financial support the client can get.

Typically, we see non-admitted companies become a solution in high catastrophe areas and for consumers with a bad claims history. When working with a non-admitted company, pay attention to the company's financial rating to get a better understanding of their financial stability and ability to pay for damages at time of a loss.

FACTORS TO CONSIDER WHEN INSURING YOUR HOME

What Type of Home Do You Have?

Single Family: The home is built for one family to live in. It is important to talk to your advisor if you live in a multigenerational home. Most insurance companies want to be informed about all household members, and there may be limited coverage for certain people based on how and who the policy considers a covered household member.

There are also types of single-family homes that require a little more attention when looking for the right coverages. For example, not all companies are comfortable with earth homes, log cabins, and "barndominiums."

Multifamily: These are locations with two or more housing units. Typically, on the personal lines side, the maximum number of units written is a fourplex. Once the structure exceeds four units, coverage goes onto a commercial policy.

Condominium: It is *all* about the bylaws. With condos, the bylaws dictate what type of coverage is needed as condos are part of an association that carries a master policy, and clients need to make sure their condo policy is in compliance with the condo bylaws.

What happens if you're in a condo and your bathroom leaks into neighbors' units, causing a lot of damage? Do you have enough liability to cover that? Or are you even responsible for the damages? Some condo bylaws restrict unit owners from pursuing other unit owners in the building for damage.

Townhome: Like condos, there are usually common areas that are insured by a master insurance policy. The difference is that with a townhome, you could be responsible for the exterior as well as the interior of your home. It is important to know what you are responsible for when owning a townhome/row house as it changes the policy form between HO-6 (interior-only coverage) or HO-3/HO-5 (which covers exterior and interior) of the home.

Location, Location, Location

Your home's location is a key consideration when designing your program. Important factors to consider when designing your program include:

1. **Does the location increase loss exposure?** Is it located on a hill, near water with hurricanes, in a wildfire area, or situated on bluffs? Maybe it is in the middle of nowhere so you can get away from the hustle and bustle of city life. These factors all increase the risk of loss, which makes them important considerations when insuring and purchasing a home.

   Hidden Risk: Typically, coverages exclude landslides. If your home sits on a hill or near water, you could experience a large financial loss if your home is damaged due to the land sliding around or under it.

   Example: The Lake of the Ozarks in Missouri is a lake with no natural water runoffs. Luxurious homes line its shore, and top-end speed boats fly up and down the lake. Since the water has nowhere to run as the waves are created, it bounces off the bluff. Erosion has begun to occur. Eventually, homes will begin to shift due to the land sliding around them. Most homeowners do not have the proper insurance for the damage to the home and potentially the liability if gas or sewage leak into the lake base of the landslide.

2. **Does the location increase the build cost?** Consider this when looking at purchase price verses replacement cost: Is it difficult to access the location? Does reaching the property involve travel over narrow gravel roads? Is the structure on uneven ground, making rebuilding more difficult? Is the build in the middle of nowhere, which increases the cost of delivering items and finding quality workers? Or are there other homes and structures close by? What is or isn't around the home makes a big difference at time of repair or rebuild.

3. **Where is the nearest fire department?** While most people don't think about this when buying or building a home, it is extremely important for insurability purposes. The proximity of the fire department and the closest fire hydrant matter. Typically, the fire station needs to be within five miles and a fire hydrant within 1,000 feet for no red flags to pop up for underwriting. This doesn't mean if your home falls outside of these parameters it is uninsurable—just that additional underwriting questions will be asked.

    Sample questions that may be asked if the building falls outside the above parameters include:
    - Where would fire crews access water should a fire occur? Or does the responding fire department have water haulers that bring water on-site?
    - Are the firefighters paid or volunteer?
    - Are roads accessible all year round?
    - What is the response time for the fire department to get to the specific address?

    Did you know? Some insurance companies offer wildfire defense coverage to help protect homes in high wildfire areas. These services range but can consist of:
    - Companies entering a fire site and rescuing valuables before a fire gets too close;
    - Removing flammable material (gas, oils, etc.) from the location of a second home to reduce the risk that some of these could cause or accelerate a fire; and/or,
    - A third party spraying a fire-retardant foam around the home to help keep the fire away from the structure itself.

4. **The number of unprotected or high fire-protection class homes** (PC8–PC10) matters. Companies want a balanced portfolio, so if you love to be secluded, make sure you understand the fire protection or you could be stuck spreading your coverages out based on companies' risk tolerance and not what's best for your protection.

5. **What natural catastrophes is the location prone to?** You need to know this because this is where one of the largest financial losses can come into play, as typically, companies have limited to no coverage for catastrophe-type losses. If there is coverage, it is with a high deductible, which means you are taking on a large chunk of the loss. With the increase we've seen in most catastrophes, it is important to work with a broker who can help find coverage for these needs. Some companies do not offer catastrophe coverages because they can't handle the financial losses if they occur. A broker can spread your risk to different markets if necessary. That way, you can have coverage for large financial losses that could be caused by one of the following:

   - **Earthquake:** They are becoming increasingly frequent, and coverage for this exposure really spreads across the U.S. This is a risk to consider based on where you live. The deductible for earthquakes is a percentage ranging from 5% to 25%, typically. It is important to understand if this deductible is applied to the total loss or to each line item (home, personal property, loss of use). Some states, such as California, have pool-provided coverage to allow clients with a specific homeowners insurance company to qualify for earthquake coverage. The California Earthquake Authority (CEA) is made up of a handful of insurance companies that has included Safeco, AAA, Farmers, Nationwide, and USAA and allows them to offer earthquake coverage at an affordable rate to their customers.

- **Flood:** FEMA has designated zones, and those zones are continually changing. If you have a loan on a home in a flood zone, you will be required to have flood insurance. The flood zone determines the cost of flood insurance, which can sometimes be substantial, ranging from $3,000 to six figures or more a year with limited market options [typically offering the National Flood Insurance Program (NFIP), which is government run]. If a home is not in a flood zone, you should still consider flood coverage. Flooding is occurring in places people never thought possible. Flood damage is defined as ground water that enters the home through doors or windows causing damage. The NFIP coverage is a limited policy; however, the private market for flood protection can offer more robust coverages for features like finished basements and loss of use.

- **Sinkhole:** While people tend to associate Florida with sinkholes, we are seeing them occur all around the U.S. For example, Missouri, Texas, Alabama, Pennsylvania, and Tennessee are also prone to sinkholes due to the geology and soil composition in certain areas.

- **Hurricane:** Hurricanes have increased dramatically in the last few years, which means we are going to start seeing changes in insurance policies in coastal states to increase deductibles and limit or remove specific coverages from policies. The difference between wind and hurricane damage is based on whether the National Hurricane Center or the National Weather Service "named" the storm. There is also verbiage in the homeowners policy specific to the speed of the wind, in which case the speed could trigger the hurricane deductible.

- **Wind:** Over the years, damage caused by wind has increased, and companies have started to limit coverage. A lot of companies have accomplished this by adding a percent deductible to the policies to help transfer some of the cost to repair or replace damages back to clients. This is an important detail to consider when comparing different coverages, as it does vary by company.

- **Hail:** The size of the hail will determine the type of damage that is done. Typically, anything under a quarter size causes cosmetic damage, whereas once the hail is larger, there is the possibility of it causing damage that compromises the integrity of the roof or siding. If the hail damage is cosmetic, do not file a claim. Consumers have become dependent on insurance companies to fix or repair their roof every time a hailstorm occurs. This isn't necessary and should be taken care of out of pocket. When buying insurance, it is important to understand how hail damage is paid and if there is a separate deductible.

6. In areas with hurricanes and strong winds, a **wind mitigation survey** is something to consider when purchasing homes in states like Florida and Texas. The survey examines a home's features that help reduce damage it may suffer because of strong winds or hurricane. There are typically seven different requirements that qualify for different discounts. The key to qualifying for any of the following is proper documentation.

- Building code: Every state looks at these requirements a little differently. In Florida, the home must be built after March 1, 2022.
- Roof must meet Florida Building Code requirements.
- Decking attachment outlines how the decking must be installed with a certain-sized nail (typically 8d).
- Roof-to-wall attachments are straps that hold the roof structure to the walls of the home.

- Roof geometry: To qualify, you must usually have some slope to your roof, which is referred to as a "hip" or "gable" shaped roof as opposed to a flat roof.
- Secondary Water Resistance (SWR) is a second layer of roof decking that is water resistant to help limit interior water damage if shingles are damaged or come off during strong winds.
- Open protection: This discount applies to windows (including doors) and shutters that are impact rated, typically with a "large missile impact rating."

Home Sweet Home? Home Away from Home? Income Stream?

Next, consider how you'll be using the home.

1. A primary residence is the home you reside in most of the time.

2. A secondary residence is any home you will reside in some portion of the year. Second homes bring different risk and risk mitigation considerations than your primary home.

   Things to consider:

   - What do you do to secure the home when you are not there? Are there any alarms, cameras, a live-in caretaker, or other loss prevention measures in place? If so, this can help reduce the cost for this home and prevent losses from occurring.

   - Do you maintain the heat at 50 degrees or shut the water off when you're not living there? If not, there could be an exclusion in your policy for water damage, so make sure to see if this applies.

   - What do you use the property for? The use of this property can drastically change the eligibility. Talk with your advisor about the fun, moneymaking, or laid-back times you have there.

3. If using the home as rental income, then there needs to be an endorsement added to the homeowners form, or it will need to be rewritten to a different policy form known as a Dwelling Fire form. There are three types of Dwelling Fire policies: Basic Form (DP1), Broad Form (DP2), and Special Form (DP3); however, not all forms are written the same. The coverages within the policy can change based on company and state. Therefore, it is extremely important to work with an informed insurance advisor to make sure you understand what you are purchasing.

    Example: I had a client in a state whose DP1 was fire coverage only. You read that right—the *only* loss the insurance would pay out for was fire damage, and the client was paying $2,000 a year for this. This was a solid brick home, so while a fire could cause some damage, the client was more likely to experience water damage (burst pipe, water backup in the basement) or hail damage—none of which were covered.

    - **DP1:** This is an actual cash value form that has a list of covered losses in the policy. This is a very limited policy, and sometimes we see only one or two types of losses covered such as fire and lightning.

    - **DP2:** This form is called "named perils," which only covers the losses listed within the policy. Per the ISO form, there are 16 covered losses:

        1: Fire or lightning
        2: Wind and hail
        3: Explosion
        4: Riot or civil commotion
        5: Aircraft
        6: Vehicle
        7: Smoke

8: Falling object

9: Damage by burglars

10: Volcanic eruption

11: Sudden and accidental tearing apart, cracking,
      burning, or bulging

12: Freezing

13: Sudden and accidental damage from arterially
      generated electrical current

14: Vandalism or malicious mischief

15: Weight of ice, snow, or sleet

16: Accidental discharge or overflow of water or steam

This covers the home on a replacement cost but personal property on an actual cash value basis.

- **DP3:** This is a replacement cost policy for the dwelling and can include items like personal property (stove, refrigerator, washer/dryer), loss of rents, and has other endorsements such as earthquake, water backup, and personal injury.

Note: It is extremely important that you read your specific policy as coverages and exclusions are specific to each company and the above is general information.

Here are some other considerations if renting to others:

- **Coverages:**

  - Include coverage for business incomes/loss of rental income, which will protect your financial loss of income if the tenant cannot live in the home due to a covered loss and is no longer paying you rent.

  - Increased liability: Always buy the maximum coverage offered, which usually is $500,000 or $1 million on a personal lines policy.

- Tenants obtaining renters policy: There are many reasons why landlords should require their tenants to carry renters insurance, to not only protect the tenant's personal property but also to provide liability. If a loss occurs because of the tenant's negligence, their renters liability would pay out.

  Example: A tenant leaves a candle burning while she goes to run a few errands and her animal knocks it over, catching the unit on fire. While your dwelling fire policy could cover this loss (it would be a chargeable loss[1] to the landlord for 3 to 5 years), if the tenant had renters insurance, the landlord's insurance company would make a claim against (or subrogate) the renters insurance policy for the cost of the claim. If the subrogation is successful, the landlord would not see this claim as chargeable on their policy.

- Underwriters factor in **how long the tenants will be in the home** and use the following categories to determine cost:

  - Annual rental: The tenants plan to use your house as their home on a yearly basis.

  - Midterm rental: The tenant is usually in the home longer than a month but not a full year. Usually these tenants are ones who travel for their profession, such as travel nurses.

  - Short-term rental: Airbnb and Vrbo are examples of short-term rentals. If you are going to offer short-term rental either in your primary home, secondary home, or rental property, it is important to disclose this to your advisor as endorsements need to be added to policies for coverage to apply if a loss occurs while the home is being rented.

---

1 "Chargeable loss" will increase the policyholder's future premium calculations.

- Will you allow your tenants to keep or bring animals?
  - Certain dog breeds and exotic animals can make your liability coverage ineligible if they cause damage or loss.
  - It is also important for short-term rentals that if you do allow animals, you make sure the tenant's homeowners coverage extends liability to other premises in case the animals damage your property or cause any sort of loss.

- **Vacant Homes:** Most home policies have vacancy clauses that go into effect once the home has been vacant for 30 to 60 days. If a home will be vacant for a long period, you will want to purchase a specific vacant home policy to cover it. The type of policy form varies from company to company.

If a loved one passed away or moves out of their home permanently, it is extremely important to contact the homeowner's company. The vacancy as well as a change of name on the deed could void the policy altogether.

- **Homes Under Renovation:** The extent of your renovation will determine the effects on your policy while your home is undergoing work. If you are thinking about doing renovations, call your advisor.

A few considerations:
  - Will you be staying at home or moving out during the renovation? Moving out typically triggers extra security requirements to help account for the increased risk of the home's vacancy during renovations.
  - Will you be using a professional to complete the work? It is important to use an insured general contractor to do the work, which transfers some of the risk back to the business for items like workers' compensation and liability.

Often if a bid is significantly lower than others, the low-bidding company does not have the overhead of insurance. While such a contractor may seem cheaper up front, doing business with such an outfit could cost you a lot more on the back end. Before you sign a contract, ask to see evidence of insurance listing the general liability limits along with confirmation of workers' compensation.

– Do *not* sign a waiver of subrogation. This takes a lot of the liability off the contractor and puts it back onto you.

Example: A lot of waivers will stipulate that if your homeowners policy covers the type of loss that it will be covered by the homeowners, and you can't come after a contractor for the damage. Here's an example of why you want to avoid signing this kind of waiver: Imagine one day a contractor leaves an oil rag on the floor in front of a window at the job site. The sun beating on the rag causes it to catch fire, leading the entire house to catch fire. The loss could be covered by the client's homeowners insurance as the ensuing damage (fire, in this case) is a covered loss. However, since it was the contractor's negligence, the client would want the contractor's liability to pay for the damage. That way, the claim is not chargeable to the client. If the client signed a waiver of subrogation, the homeowner's company would not be able to subrogate back to the general contractor. Some insurance companies will not continue coverage if you sign a waiver of subrogation because they do not want to take on that additional exposure of the contractor's and subcontractor's negligence.

- Most insurance companies have clauses that state if you do not notify them before work starts, coverage is void or a higher deductible such as 5% can apply to losses.

- Confirm contractors have completed background checks on their employees.

- Will you be adding square footage or updating an existing structure? Will you be removing any load-bearing walls? These are types of renovations that need to be discussed with your advisor before work is started as there may need to be a builder-risk policy put into place, depending on the amount of square footage added.

- What type of security will you have in place during renovation? Will there be extra fire extinguishers or cameras on-site if you're not living there? Will ladders be put away once the crew leaves for the day? Will you post "No Smoking on the Job" signs? Will oil rags be stored in a fire-safe container? There will be some safety requirements from the insurance company but also precautions homeowners should consider, helping avoid a loss while upgrading their home.

Determine if a contactor has coverage and why you should care.

First and foremost, as stated above, request a current *certificate of insurance* showing workers' compensation and general liability coverages are in effect with the official bid they submit for you to review. Depending on the job, you may also want to confirm they are bonded.

- **Consider this:** You decide to upgrade your kitchen and get a few bids. The first offer comes in at $25,000 from a big-name company that can get it done in your time frame. The second offer comes in at $23,000 but will take a little longer than you want as it's a one-man shop but with insurance. The third offer of $20,000 comes from a contractor who has no insurance. If he gets hurt (workers' compensation) or damages your home in the process (general liability with right endorsements), you will have a big problem on your hands. The third outfit can submit a lower bid because they do not have the overhead cost of insurance. Choosing option one or two, even though they are slightly higher, will give you greater peace of mind. Just make sure they have insurance. While the up-front savings with the third contractor is tempting, the possibility of footing a bigger bill is more than likely because you are taking on the risk of paying the contractor's or his workers' medical bills and lost wages if they are injured on your property.

- **Example:** While finishing up the kitchen and doing the final paint job, the contractor slips off the ladder. He is seriously injured, needing surgery, rehab, and months off work (maybe never returning). Since you opted for the cheaper bid and the contractor who did not have insurance, you're left holding the bag when your dog runs by and knocks him off the ladder. You are now responsible for his medical bills, lost wages, and potential change in lifestyle of about $650,000. How would you pay for that? And was the $5,000 up-front savings truly worth it?
  Note: There can be exclusions in personal liability (home and umbrella) that remove liability coverages for people working on premises. If that exclusion is in the client's homeowners insurance policy, they could be responsible for coming up with the $650,000 personally.

- **Farm** is a broad term, and the use of the land will determine if the home can be written on a standard homeowners form or if it should be written on a farm policy.

  Hobby Farm: These farms usually do not maintain animals, or if they do, they are leisure animals such as horses for family fun (rather than those ridden in competitive shows or racing). It is important to discuss all aspects of the "farm" as there are some triggering activities that cause eligibility issues with companies.

  A few considerations:

  Business or hobby activities that create income should be discussed with your advisor as there are different dollar amounts that trigger eligibility and determine whether the location can be written on a personal lines form or a commercial farm policy.

  What **type of animals** will be housed in the location, and what activities will take place there?

  - **Hunting:** If you are charging a fee for people to come onto your land, then you are running a business that needs to be on a commercial policy. If only friends and family are using the land to hunt, then typically it's okay to be designated as a hobby farm.

  - **Sharecropping:** If the client is the individual leasing the land to the farmer, it is important to understand the contract between the "farmer" and "landowner" as that will determine who is responsible for insuring the crops. This situation can be murky and depends upon the contract. Some homeowners forms permit this, whereas others require the farm be on a commercial policy because of the activities taking place (even though the insured is not the one who is farming).

- Will you be running a **business out of the home**? If yes, this could also raise eligibility concerns as there is limited or no coverage for business property on a homeowners form. Talk with your advisor about your specific risk. Homeowners policies do *not* cover business exposures, so it is important that clients have the proper commercial coverage(s) in place to cover the business entity and its activities.

Considerations if you run a business out of your home:

- Do clients come onto the premises? If yes, this increases your liability exposure of someone being hurt at your home and sometimes can make you ineligible with certain insurance companies.

- Do you run a daycare or animal care out of your home? Running a business with people's loved ones as clients on your premises not only increases your liability but also changes the exposure and losses you may face. Clients must discuss these types of activities with the homeowner's insurance company.

  Example: I once had a client who wanted to run a dog-sitting business out of their home because they loved dogs. They didn't need the money, and it was more of a hobby. However, this caused major issues with underwriting because there were going to be different dogs (and breeds) on the premises at all times of day. The chances of a dog bite or damages occurring to the home because of the dog(s) the client was caring for was too much for the company to feel comfortable with.

  The only homeowners option we found was for **surplus lines coverage through a non-admitted company** that excluded animal liability. My professional opinion was to not pursue the business and to find another way to fulfill their passion. This is because by not having liability coverage for the animals they would have as pets or care for, the insured was taking on a large risk, one that would outweigh the cost of doing business. For example, what if a friend visits and is confronted by an unknown dog who is also scared in a new place? The dog bites your friend, causing $30,000 in medical bills that you as the homeowner are now responsible for because your homeowners insurance excludes coverage for a dog bite.

The client also lost a lot of other coverages, including earthquake, full limit water backup, and top-notch claims service by moving from a high-net-worth insurance company to a surplus lines company to run this business.

Who Owns the Home?

When an advisor asks who the **named insured** on the policy should be, you need to think about the title of the property. Is the home in the name of a trust, LLC, or family member? How a property is titled can affect who can be the name insured.

In addition, it is extremely important that the deed and named insured match at time of claim. The named insured must have an insurable interest in the home for the policy to respond. If the named insured and deed do not match, the insurance company could deny the claim.

The next thing to consider is if you title your home in any name other than your personal name. You will want to make sure that you as an individual are listed on the policy as well as your trust, LLC, etc. This is important because the insurance coverage only responds to the named insured and additional named insured on the policy.

Example: You transfer the title of your home into a trust and update the deed to reflect that. If you do not contact your homeowner's insurance company and there is a liability loss at the home, you would hire an attorney to protect your trust during the claim. The insurance company only has a duty to defend the insured named on the policy, and if the trust is not listed, they could deny coverage to the trust. Some insurance companies automatically include coverage for additional insureds like trust, LLC, etc. It's better to be safe than sorry, so call and add it! On the flip side, it's not always beneficial to write the homeowners policy only in the name of the trust or LLC. This is because then you, as an individual, won't have certain coverage, like liability. You also could lose personal property coverage unless you plan to have all personal property placed in trust (which is advisable but often overlooked).

Solution: Write the policy in your personal name and add trust or LLC as an additional insured on the policy.

Is Anyone Helping You Maintain Your Lifestyle?

Whether it's a cleaning service, landscapers, nannies or au pairs, a butler, or bartenders hired for a gathering, if you are paying someone to help work on *your* property for a service, you could be considered their employer at time of loss. This is important because, in some states, if you are found liable, you could be stuck with their medical bill, lost wages, future wages, lump sum settlement, etc. You might think, "Isn't that what my homeowners is for?" No, because the people who work on your premises should carry their own coverages for the business/work they are completing. If you are their only employer, such as with an au pair or house manager, then it is your responsibility to get workers' compensation and other coverages to protect you and your employee in the course of their job. If not and they are injured, and you are responsible, where are you going to get the funds? Savings, investments, future earnings?

In today's world, insurance is not only used to address people who become injured. What if one of your employees feels discriminated against, sexually harassed, or wrongfully terminated? Do you have the right coverages to protect yourself? Most people do not as there are only a handful of companies that offer protection for these situations on the personal lines side. Usually, we see this coverage provided via employment practice liability on a personal umbrella. Or it can be purchased on the commercial side where there is a large market for these coverages, which may be necessary depending on the size of your staff.

How to limit your risk:

1. Hire companies or individuals who carry their own insurance: both workers' compensation and general liability insurance.

2. You need to purchase workers' compensation insurance, employers' liability, employment practices liability, and other insurance to transfer the risk if you are the employer.

What Is Your Home Made of? Why Replacement Cost Is Important

Replacement cost, aka dwelling value or the rebuild cost, *is not* market value. When designing your homeowners program, do *not* use the purchase price of your home as the insurance dwelling value.

You need to consider the specifics that make your home yours when coming up with the replacement cost for your structure. The custom kitchen, bathrooms, painted ceilings, wine cellar, in-home gym, finished basement, and any other personal upgrades will help you and your advisor determine the replacement cost. If you don't take these factors into account in initial discussions, you could be out a lot of money at time of loss, and it will cost you to "upgrade" your home back to its original status.

You can purchase endorsements such as extended replacement cost or guaranteed replacement cost. The extended replacement cost ranges from 20%

to 100%, and this is the amount you'd get in addition to the dwelling limit listed on the declarations. Guaranteed means the insurance company will pay whatever it takes to replace your home at time of loss.

- This coverage is important should there be a catastrophe such as a tornado or hurricane and the cost of labor and lumber skyrocket due to supply and demand. The replacement cost is usually calculated for only your home being affected, rather than an entire area. For example, a fire caused by lightning would not result in a surge in supply and demand.

- We've also seen this come into play during the 2020 pandemic where cost of labor and lumber increased because of shortage in supply.

- Do not rely on the extended replacement cost to get you to the true replacement cost. Let's say the true replacement cost to rebuild a home is $450,000. You cannot insure the home for $375,000 with 20% extended replacement cost to get you to the $450,000 because that is the max you will get, and you will most likely be underinsured at time of a large loss.

Coinsurance: If you have a replacement cost policy but your home is not insured to replacement cost, you could run into a coinsurance[2] issue at time of loss. This means you won't get the full cost it takes to replace the damage regardless of what the declaration page states for dwelling coverage. Most policies require 80% or 100% insurance to value, and this is specifically stated in your insurance contract.

The **coinsurance equation** is easy—the **coverage you have** *divided by* the **dwelling coverage** you should have had *times* **the loss amount = the payout**.

---

2 Generally, coinsurance is applied to the portion of the rebuild cost, which is transferred back to the consumer. If coinsurance is included, it is usually defined as a percentage in the policy. Coinsurance allows you to take on more risk associated with rebuild costs to reduce the premium.

Example: Let's say when you purchase your home, you call the local agent and insure your home for the purchase price of $899,000. Over the summer, you leave for a weeklong vacation and return to your home being covered in water because of a busted pipe on the second floor, causing $200,000 in damages. When the adjuster comes out to inspect the home, the cost to rebuild the home is closer to $1.4 million, and there is a coinsurance clause of 100% in the homeowners policy. This means for the insurance company to pay 100% of the loss, the home must be insured to 100% replacement cost value of $1.4 million, which it was not. So now the adjuster is going to use the above formula: 899,000 / 1,400,000 x 200,000 = $128,428, which is the total the client will get for the loss because of the coinsurance penalty. In addition to the deductible you chose, you are out another $80,000 because the home was not insured to value. It is *extremely* important to know if there is a coinsurance clause in your home policy and, if there is, how the advisor determined the replacement cost.

With a **custom home** comes custom features and coverages to consider. Here are a few:

- Do you use your basement for storage? Is the basement finished? Regardless of the purpose, if you have a basement, you should have water backup coverage (this can also be referred to as "escape of water" and other terms depending on the company). This coverage kicks in should water back up into the home (typically through drains) but can also be toilets or bathtubs (usually sewage) due to water backing up. If you have a basement and use it for storage or additional living, the coverage needs vary. This is another coverage where limits vary from company to company, with some maxing out at $25,000 and other insurance companies offering 100% of the dwelling replacement cost in backup limits. All homeowners should have no less than $10,000 in water backup regardless of having a basement or not.

- Did you purchase a fixer-upper? The purchase price and the new replacement cost may be drastically different. Consider all the blood, sweat, and tears you put into it. Would you really want to redo it? If you carry the right replacement cost, you will not have to do it again because the replacement cost also takes labor cost into account. That means you can hire a team of professionals to make you whole.

- Maybe you spent years working with a custom builder to design the home of your dreams with such amenities as imported marble in the bathroom, an in-home theater, heated floors, an all-season room, and his and hers closets. Building a home from the ground up is different from rebuilding/fixing a damaged home, and this should be reflected in your replacement cost.

- If you have a smart home, consider the right cyber protection.

- Did you purchase a home that was in a neighborhood with other custom homes that have similar floor plans? The cost to build those new is usually less than replacement cost because those builders get bulk pricing discounts for using similar building materials for multiple job sites.

Take a Step Outside Your Home. What Do You See?

While some people purchase a home for the interior, others fall in love with the outdoor living. From a stunning landscape to a pool, outdoor kitchen, skate ramps, trampoline, zipline, animals, or a playground, the exterior of a home can make your heart skip a beat but can add a lot of risk to consider when creating a homeowners program. In general, your outdoor living and structures will be covered by "Other Structures" in your homeowners policy. This limit is typically a percent of your dwelling value, so make sure to adjust the limit accordingly. Your personal liability also needs to be reviewed based on what is in your backyard.

- The stunning landscape from front to back: There is a limit in your standard homeowners policy (typically $5,000) for *all* landscape. Are those old oaks that you love so much replaceable? If so, what would the cost be to purchase a mature tree to replace it at time of loss? What is the cost to remove one of the large oak trees if it falls? Tree removal is another limited coverage in most home protection programs.

- The pool you love adds an additional liability risk. Anyone with a pool should have a minimum of a $1 million umbrella. You also need to make sure you limit your liability risk by having a locked fence around the pool. A lot of insurance companies now require this to offer a policy. The slide and diving board your kids begged you for increase the risk of someone getting hurt. Some companies will not even offer liability if the pool includes a slide.

  If you have a party, consider hiring a lifeguard to manage the pool to ensure everyone's safety and limit your liability.

- If your home has an outdoor kitchen, make sure the cost of that is considered in the other structure limit.

- If your home has a dock (boat dock, swimming dock, party dock), make sure you also consider its cost in your other structures. There are some exclusions such as weight of ice and snow that could affect you if you have a dock exposure in a state that gets cold. This coverage can be purchased back with some companies and is something to talk through based on the dock's location.

- While home playgrounds are fun, the right liability coverage needs to be considered if you have one—66% of all playground losses occurred at an individual's home, according to the U.S. Consumer Product Safety Commission (CPSC).

- Animals can be the apple of our eyes, and sometimes their homes (barns) are as nice, or nicer, than ours. Make sure you discuss your animals and their structures when reviewing your program. Also, the insurance companies assess animals as part of their underwriting. If you have animals, you will want to discuss with your advisor what coverage, if any, you have for them and the liability they bring.

- Don't forget the hardscape. Retaining walls are not inexpensive, and the cost of repairing or replacing hardscape can be a major cost overlooked in planning.

Whatever your backyard oasis is, make sure to consult with your personal risk advisor whenever making changes or upgrades. The cost needs to be considered in the other structure coverage of your policy, and the increased risk exposure needs to be evaluated. Maybe the change at your home is an exclusion in your home policy, like a slide on your pool. And if someone gets hurt because of that slide, your claim could be denied. You will then have to hire an attorney and shell out your hard-earned money to pay for the individual's medical bills, lost wages, pain and suffering, etc. This could be avoided with the right planning and a phone call to your advisor to make sure you have the proper coverage in place.

Risk Mitigation: Who Really Has Time for a Claim?

Risk mitigation is what is used to avoid a claim from occurring or lessen the severity of the loss. A few of the common mitigation tools that also receive additional discounts on your homeowners include:

- Security cameras monitored by a third party: If they have signal continuity, you'll get an additional discount.

- Water shutoff: There are a few versions of these devices. Some have alarms, and others will shut off the water to your home if a leak is detected. The monitoring service and the capabilities of the water device will determine the size of credit added to the home. This is a *great* addition to any home, especially vacation homes or homes not occupied on a regular basis. Water damage is one of the top causes of loss to homeowners.

- Background checks on employees before you allow them to work for you: Unfortunately, most in-home theft occurs from employees because clients get comfortable leaving valuables out or sharing valuable information.

- Infrared inspections are a service add-on with some of the high-net-worth companies. These are very beneficial for homeowners as they can detect moisture behind the walls, missing or limited insulation, and other potential losses lurking behind the walls.

- Backup generators are not only nice to have but can help protect some of your most valuable assets if the electricity goes out—keeping the sump pump running, the temperature correct for the wine storage, or maintaining the status quo even during a storm.

- Sump pumps help limit the possibility of water backup into your home. It is important to have a backup battery for the sump pump as ones powered only by electricity will be useless if the electricity goes out during a big rainstorm.

- A temperature monitor can be added to a central alarm station and will notify the client if the temperature within the home drops to a certain level to help keep pipes from freezing or potentially detect a fire if the temperature rises drastically.

Flexibility at Time of Claim

Filing a claim can be one of the worst days of your life. If you find yourself in this challenging situation, it can be beneficial to have options for putting yourself and your life back together. Some affluent insurance companies offer:

- **Waiver of deductible:** If the claim goes over a certain dollar amount, a waiver of deductible will go into effect. Currently that amount is $50,000, but we do see insurance companies increasing this limit in the coming years as the $50,000 limit was established decades ago.

- **Cash-out option:** This attractive option is not talked about enough. Most clients think they have this coverage, but in reality, they do not. With a cash-out option, if your home experiences a total loss, you can take the dwelling value and walk away with the face value in cash and not be stuck rebuilding. You may have to leave the premises in compliance with local or state regulations, which can be covered depending on your policy form. This is beneficial for multiple reasons:

  - What happens if your community does not rebuild? Do you want to be living in the only home there? Maybe the school district doesn't come back. Having flexibility to move at time of loss is key.

  - Maybe life is in transition—having kids, kids moving out, downsizing for retirement. The life reasons are many, and the option to buy a home elsewhere without being locked into rebuilding a home you may no longer want or need allows life to move on much more smoothly.

- **Choice of contractor:** While most insurance allows you to choose with whom you work, sometimes the policy language and the wrong limits can limit the budget you have versus the true cost and needs to repair. With the right coverages, you will be able to choose the right contractors and artisans to rebuild and repair your home. Be prepared when going with a cost-effective policy to have cost-effective repairs.

As outlined above, every part of your home and your day-to-day life is important when designing your homeowners insurance policy coverage. Two big takeaways: (1) Don't assume it's covered, and (2) consult with a professional to help you make the right decisions.

Chapter 3:

Auto Insurance

Whether you own, rent, or ride in a car, you need auto insurance. By owning a vehicle, you are legally required to carry some form of auto liability coverage. The minimum requirement varies by state. If you do not own a vehicle but rent or ride in a vehicle, you also have an exposure that is typically covered by a nonowned auto policy. And don't forget about the recreational toys in your life. Don't just assume there is coverage for these items—even something as ordinary as a bike.

Auto insurance basics are straightforward in terms of available coverages. But how the vehicle is used, its value, who is driving the vehicle, and why they are driving it can complicate how coverage is applied, if at all, at time of a loss.

LIABILITY

There are two ways to purchase liability coverage on an auto policy: split limit or combined single limits. Typically, people carry split limits. That's because with the mass markets, it is cheaper, but there are also per-person and property damage caps within that policy. The combined single limit policy removes the per-person cap and lumps the property damage into the total available liability limit.

The first liability limits on an auto policy are bodily injury and property damage, which pays out to the other person if you are found at fault for a loss.

First liability limits are typically listed with a per-person limitation / per-accident limitation / limitation for property damage sustained. Limitations vary and can range widely. For example:

- $500,000 (per person) / $500,000 (per accident) / $500,000 (property damage);

- $250,000 (per person) / $500,000 (per accident) / $100,000 (property damage);

- $100,000 (per person) / $300,000 (per accident) / $50,000 (property damage); and so on.

Options vary by company and state.

Claims Example: One rainy day while driving down the highway, you look down for a split second then look back up and see the BMW ahead of you stopping. You hit the brakes and slide into the BMW's rear. The brand-new BMW is a total loss and will cost $134,000 to replace. In addition, the car's driver was injured, going to the hospital by ambulance and spending time in the hospital, resulting in missed work and pain and suffering due to the collision. The other driver's total medical bill and lost wages due to the accident are $300,000.

- **Coverage under a split limit policy:** You have an auto policy with $250,000 per person / $500,000 per accident with $100,000 in property damage. For this accident, you would be underinsured as the per-person cap is $250,000 and the bills were $300,000, leaving you $50,000 out of pocket for medical bills/lost wages, and then another $34,000 for the vehicle as your property damage cap was $100,000. In total, this loss would cost you $84,000 out of pocket before the pain and suffering claim comes into the equation.

The other way liability is listed is a combined single limit, which removes the per-person cap and the property damage limit and gives you one "bucket" of money known as the acident limit at time of a claim.

- **Coverage under a combined single limit policy:** You have an auto policy with $500,000 in liability per accident. For this accident, the entire claim would be covered by your auto insurance because the $300,000 in medical bills plus the $134,000 in property damage is $434,000, which is under your $500,000 limit.

Hidden Risk: You are probably wondering whether the other person's health insurance would cover this accident. When an individual goes to a doctor or hospital, one of the first questions is "How did the injury occur?" When the injured party responds that they were in an auto accident, the liability/responsibility shifts to you, the driver. And that is why you purchase auto insurance because part of your liability coverage pays for this expense (medical bills). In some states, you are not only held responsible for immediate damages but also the above-mentioned pain/suffering and other changes of life caused by the accident.

Uninsured and underinsured liability coverage (UM/UIM) is the next layer of coverage. This can also be purchased in a split limit or combined single limit. On average, one in seven drivers have no auto insurance. It's important to carry the right limit and not "save money" and take on this very foreseeable risk. These UM/UIM liability limits are what pay out to you and your family if you are hit by someone who has no insurance or not enough to pay for your lost wages, medical bills, and change in your quality of life. This limit also does more than just protect you while in a vehicle; it can also extend to you while you are riding a bike for pleasure or walking.

Hidden Risk: Every state requires minimum liability coverage that the state sets, which varies by state. This is the bare minimum coverage someone needs to legally drive on the road. Do not think that these minimum limits will do much to help make you whole again if the accident is more than a minor fender bender. A handful of states have minimum coverage of $25,000 per person / $50,000 per accident/ $15,000 in property damage. However, a few states only require property damage and personal injury protection with requirements as low as $5,000 in property damage and $10,000 in personal injury protection.

In some states, you can buy UM/UIM coverage with add-on liability or limit coverage with reduced limits for UM/UIM. If you live in a state where you do not have the option to buy add-on coverage, you most likely automatically have reduced limits. Here's what that means:

Claims Example: Let's say you are hit by someone and have $750,000 in medical bills, lost wages, and change in lifestyle. The party that hit you has a split limit policy with a $250,000 per-person cap.

- Add-on limit, aka stacked liability limits: The entire claim would be covered as the $250,000 in coverage they have plus the $500,000 in uninsured and underinsured liability you have would total $750,000 and would cover your loss.

- Reduced limit: This entire claim would *not* be covered as their $250,000 limit reduces your $500,000 by $250,000, which only pays you a total of $500,000 for this claim. In this situation, you'd be stuck suing the other party for the additional cost or you could purchase additional limits on your umbrella coverage to better protect you so you are not left suing someone who may not have many resources.

Note: In addition, some states allow you to limit your future ability to sue to help save on premiums—known as limited tort. This means if the other party who injures you does not have enough insurance, you may not have the ability to sue them for additional damages over their insurance limits based on the policy you purchased. You can buy up this coverage to be zero tort (aka full tort), which does not limit your ability to sue.

The last piece of liability coverage on the auto policy is **medical payments**. There are two types of coverage that you can use within your auto policy that cover you and provide coverage to you regardless of fault.

- **Medical payment** typically helps cover medical deductibles and copays that arise out of an accident.

- **Personal injury protection** is broader coverage and only available in specific states. It covers the same costs as medical payment plus can also provide coverage for aftercare such as physical therapy and funeral expenses.

HOW IS YOUR VEHICLE COVERED?

Now that you've purchased the right liability coverage, the next part of your auto policy to consider is the physical or property damage that may occur to your vehicle. There are a few ways to cover your vehicle for physical damage.

1. **Full Coverage:** You are covered for collision and comprehensive damage. Collision is the coverage if your vehicle is damaged while moving or collides into something. The comprehensive coverage covers the vehicle while not being operated or acts of God. If you have an auto loan, you are required to carry full coverage.

2. **Comprehensive Only** (aka Other than Collision): This means if you crash your vehicle into something, there is NO coverage. Sometimes clients will opt for this coverage to keep costs down and protect them from events like hail damage or a tree branch falling on the vehicle. This is an important coverage even if your vehicle is parked or in storage.

Hidden Risk: The comprehensive deductible is what is applied at time of glass damage. Some companies allow clients to buy down the glass deductible to $0 so there is no out-of-pocket cost for the glass.

3. **Not at All:** Also known as liability-only coverage. If you are involved in an accident, you will be 100% responsible for fixing your vehicle's damage. Typically, we see this on older vehicles but have seen it when an individual is comfortable taking on the risk of repairs/replacement on any vehicle and self-insures the physical damage.

With options 1 and 2, you will need to choose your deductibles. The deductible is what you are responsible for at time of damage. The higher the deductible, the lower your auto rates will be as you are taking on more risk. Typically, we see deductibles ranging from $500 to $2,500 or more on an auto policy.

- You can choose separate dollar amounts for the comprehensive and collision deductibles. Typically, comprehensive deductibles are not major premium drivers, so we see these left lower than the collision for overall cost efficiency.

- You only pay your deductible at time of repairs to your vehicle. If you carry liability only and hit someone else's car, you want to make sure you have the correct property damage liability to cover the cost of the vehicle or other property that may be damaged.

Like homeowners insurance, choosing the right auto deductible is very important. Not all auto claims need to be filed, and filing only necessary claims to stay insurable and keep rates down is in the insured's best interest. Carrying the right deductible will help achieve both objectives.

- **Hidden Risk:** There are situations where the parties involved in an accident can work outside insurance to settle an auto claim if damages are minor and the other party has the funds to take care of the damages out of pocket. If you choose this option, consult with your advisor and get proper documents signed to release each party from any future liabilities that may arise.

- **Hidden Risk:** Another option is working with an attorney to take care of things like speeding tickets and having them moved to nonmoving violations. Speeding tickets are chargeable for 3 to 5 years and, depending on how fast the individual is going over the speed limit, could make the driver ineligible for auto and umbrella coverage in the future.

- **Hidden Risk:** There is usually no personal property coverage within your auto policy. That means that if someone breaks into your vehicle and steals your property, you'd have to file two claims: one with the auto insurance for the window/damage to the vehicle and a second claim with your homeowners insurance to pay for your stolen personal property. Sometimes it is not worth filing a separate claim on your home depending on the value of the items, your homeowners deductible, and overall impact on that premium.

  - If you are a renter, you would claim personal property stolen under your renters insurance.

  - Some companies include minimal coverage for personal property, typically around $500, which could be a nice benefit to have if you are known to leave personal items in your vehicle.

Insurance kicks in after damages exceed your deductible. When a vehicle is damaged in an auto accident, it is either repaired or deemed a total loss. At time of a total loss, there are two ways a claim can be paid out for your vehicle. The most common way is actual cash value. The second way is to buy up coverage for an agreed value.

- **Actual Cash Value (ACV)** is based on the value of your vehicle minus depreciation. Factors such as mileage and condition of vehicle matter. The maintenance is not something that typically affects the ACV.

- **Agreed Value** is an upgrade available on some policies where the insured and insurance company agree on the value of the vehicle at the start of the policy term. If there is a total loss, the claim is settled quickly since the value was already agreed upon. Agreed Value allows the client to have a little more say in the value for which the vehicle is insured.

Roadside assistance: If you have an old car, use a third-party roadside service such as an AAA membership. Roadside assistance on the auto insurance is intended to be used infrequently and mostly at time of claim. If you use the roadside assistance within your auto policy too many times, this can cause an underwriting/eligibility issue due to frequency and may potentially make you uninsurable.

Rental car coverage provides coverage for a replacement vehicle after an auto accident occurs. This is usually listed on your declaration with a per-day limit and total accident limit.

Hidden Risk: Even if you have an extra car at home, what happens if you are in an accident while on vacation and need a car while yours is being repaired? The cost is minimal and is nice to have when needed.

Additionally, consider the limit you are purchasing. If you drive a nicer vehicle, you need a minimum of $50 a day/$1,500 per accident max to get you back into a similar vehicle. If you drive a luxury vehicle, consider limits without daily caps. This is typically offered in the affluent insurance market with limits starting at $2,500 and upwards of $15,000 while your vehicle is being repaired.

When renting a car, it's important to understand how your insurance applies to the vehicle you are renting. Usually, liability can extend if you have one vehicle on your policy with full coverage. However, there are some gaps in the standard auto policy when renting a vehicle.

- Loss of use and diminishing value are typically not covered.

  - **Loss of Use Example:** You rent a vehicle and are in an accident. You happen to be in the city where there is a big event the following weekend, and the vehicle you crashed will not be able to be rented. The rental car company can come after you for the loss of rental income since the vehicle is not operational and can no longer generate income due to your accident.

  - **Diminishing Value Example:** In a similar scenario but instead of the busy weekend loss of use damages, the rental car company was planning to take the vehicle to auction to sell. Now that the vehicle has been in an accident, the value for the vehicle decreased from $37,000 to $32,000. You could be held responsible for that $5,000 difference.

- You must have full coverage on at least one of your vehicles for coverage to apply to rental.

- If you are in an accident, your auto deductible does apply to the damage.

- If you have a driver on your auto policy who no longer lives at home, there could be limited to no coverage while they are renting a vehicle, even if they are listed on the policy. Every auto policy reads differently, and it is important to understand if certain liability limits are available to only household members, listed drivers, or both.

- Who will be driving the rental car? If there will be a few different drivers, it is important to understand how insurance is applied at time of loss.

  Hidden Risk: Personal auto insurance usually follows the vehicles on the policy. Extension to rental car coverage is a limited extension, and there are restrictions that are not usually applied when driving your personal vehicle or allowing others to drive your personal vehicle with permissive use.

Original Equipment Manufacturer (OEM) parts are another endorsement that needs to be added to some auto policies to have the vehicle repaired with manufacturer parts at the time of a loss. Without this coverage, the insurance company can use aftermarket parts to repair the vehicle, which is common with most policies. When considering OEM parts, take the following into account:

- If you have a loan or lease, read the contract to see if you are required to repair with OEM parts.

- There is nothing simple about windshields anymore. From sensors to calibration, the cost to repair and replace windshields is increasing. If you want to have $0 out-of-pocket cost and all the bells and whistles on the replacement windshield, this is the coverage that is needed.

- Drivers of classic, luxury, and exotic vehicles should also consider including this protection to maintain the vehicle's quality without having to pay additional cost over the deductible at time of repair.

WHY DO YOU DRIVE YOUR CAR?

While this is a question you may not often ponder, it's extremely important to consider when crafting your personal auto policy.

Typically, there are three ways to rate a vehicle: business use, commute use, or pleasure use. It is important to choose the proper classification so the insurance company can charge the proper rate for your exposure and avoid gray areas at a time of a loss.

The language within an auto policy can exclude coverages based on how the vehicle is being used at a time of a loss. Below are a few examples of ways you may use your vehicle that could affect coverage at the time of an accident:

- Restrictions apply within a personal auto policy when using the vehicle for business. For example, if you're in sales (with no clients in the vehicle) and drive to customer sites, you have a greater chance of a claim than if you are commuting to an office. Insurance companies want to be able to rate for this increased exposure of driving, which is why the business rating is available. It is *not* intended to provide coverage when the vehicle is being used:

  - For selling, repairing, servicing, or parking vehicles;
  - To pick up and deliver people;

    If you drive for companies like Uber or Lyft, for instance, you need to understand where the company's coverage starts and ends. There is an available endorsement with most personal insurance companies for "ride sharing," which is meant to fill in some gaps in coverage that the commercial insurance policies do not cover such as the "trolling" period, which is when the insured/driver is in between riders. This endorsement is not intended to include private chauffeur driver services, which would be a commercial policy.

– Or to pick up and deliver food or other products for compensation.

If you drive for companies like Uber, GrubHub, etc., it is important to disclose this information as you may need a commercial auto policy or the proper endorsement added to your personal auto policy depending on who you are delivering for and what.

- There are now websites that enable individuals to rent their personal vehicles to the public. While the concept is interesting, it opens gray areas in coverage that can leave an individual exposed should an accident occur. Insurance companies view renting out your vehicle as a business or commercial exposure. This activity isn't covered in your typical personal auto policy.

  If you are the one renting a vehicle from a site like Turo, it is important to check with your insurance provider to see how or if coverage is extended.

Maybe you like to have fun with your vehicle. Certain activities can limit or void coverage in an auto policy. Examples of these activities include:

- Mudding (driving a vehicle off-road through wet fields, lakeshores, or other muddy areas)
- Racing
- Rock crawling
- Parades

WHO IS DRIVING YOUR VEHICLES?

Another important question to consider is who is driving the vehicles. While there can be coverage for permissive users, it does not mean coverage is treated equally. Permissive is a broad term. Depending on how often the vehicle is driven by that person, if they live in the household, etc., can change how coverage is applied.

Hidden Risk: Some insurance companies have placed limited liability within their policies when a permissive driver is operating the vehicle and an accident occurs.

Example: Your auto policy has $250,000 per person / $500,000 per accident; however, there is a clause within the policy that states if the accident occurs by a driver *not* listed on the policy, then certain limits apply (typically drops down to state minimum, which on average is $25,000 per person / $50,000 per accident / $25,000 in property damage).

Generally, permissive users are people who you give permission to use your vehicle on a limited/rare basis. However, people who use the vehicles frequently should be added on the auto policy as a driver. These include:

- Household employees: This includes a house manager, au pairs, nannies, and people who will have regular access to your vehicle.

  - If the employees will be driving their own vehicles while working for you, it is important to understand the coverages they have and if any exclusions apply while in the course of work for you. Also consider the limits they have. If your children will be in their vehicle and they carry low liability for uninsured and underinsured coverage, you could be leaving your loved ones exposed. To avoid any unknowns, request a copy of the employee's declarations and ask to be added as an additional interest so you can receive notices should there be a lapse in coverage.

- Being added as an additional interest does not open your liability; it keeps you informed about their policy being in force and sends you necessary notices.

- Employees: Perhaps you are a business owner, and you allow your assistant to drive your vehicle on a regular basis. Personal insurance policies don't cover this kind of use. Consider adding commercial auto coverage for vehicles that are regularly used by employees.

- If you have a vehicle that is not kept at your home, make sure you include the proper garaging address for the vehicle as this does factor into the rate and may affect coverage.

- If driving-age children are away at school, make sure you talk with them about who is and is not allowed to drive the vehicles. Also, reinforce the importance of keeping their car keys in a safe place.

Story: Early in my insurance career, I went to visit my two younger sisters who were part of a sorority at a major university. As I pulled up around 6 p.m. on a Friday, I noticed my sister's SUV was not in the parking lot. I called my sister to see where she was, and she told me that she was in the house and that another sorority sister was using the car to transport sorority sisters to and from town as the designated driver that night. From the outside, that sounded like a good idea; however, the risk manager in me couldn't help but think:

- What if the driver gets distracted and crashed the car full of bright, young students or if a deer jumps out of the woods? Did my parents have enough liability coverage to cover that sort of loss?

- If my parents didn't have enough liability coverage, was the vehicle title in my parents' names, and, if yes, were their assets now vulnerable? The answer could be yes. If the insurance is exhausted, my parents' assets could have been up for grabs because of a "simple" choice my sisters made and how the vehicle was titled.

– Was there something my parents could do to help limit the exposure of their assets due to underinsurance? Yes, and they did. They put the vehicle's title in my middle sister's name to help avoid the potential claim of negligent entrustment if the auto insurance became exhausted.

Note: I am not an attorney, and this is general advice, so please consult with a professional on your individual situation.

How the vehicle is titled determines who carries the liability at time of a loss. Make sure to disclose how vehicles are titled as some companies have different eligibility guidelines based on titling, especially if titled to a nonresident household member or titled in a business name.

DON'T OWN A CAR? YOU STILL NEED INSURANCE (NON-OWNED AUTO).

For those who do not own a vehicle but maybe use friends' or family's cars, take public transportation, walk, or bike around town, you still have lifestyle exposures to consider. A non-owned auto policy is what can protect your auto liability when you do not own a vehicle.

Consider this: Most companies require underlying auto insurance to qualify for an umbrella policy, and non-owned auto insurance is what can help meet those requirements when there are no vehicles in a household.

1. When renting vehicles, there is an option to carry your own liability coverage and forgo purchasing it through the rental car company. Depending on how frequently you rent a car, it could be cost-efficient to have a non-owned policy to cover you in these situations. Non-owned auto insurance also provides additional protection

like uninsured and underinsured limits that aren't always available through the rental car insurance.

2. What if you are riding your bike or your family member is walking down the street and is hit by someone who takes off after the accident or only has state minimum coverage? The non-owned policy uninsured or underinsured limits would kick in to help pay for the injuries your family sustained. Without this coverage, you could find yourself hiring (and paying for) an attorney to sue the other party who injured you (if you can find them) and hope they have the means—liquidity in their home, a good job, or other assets—that could be used to collect against to make you whole again.

3. Or maybe you're a passenger either in a friend's car or ride-sharing vehicle and you are severely injured because of the driver's negligence, and the driver's auto insurance is exhausted. In some states, the injured party can utilize their own insurance coverage (UM/UIM) to pay for the rest of the damages caused by the loss, such as change in ability to work, pain/suffering, and other life changes that result from the accident.

4. Finally, non-owned auto can help keep or build insurance history, which is beneficial in keeping your auto rates competitive if you decide to buy a vehicle.

CLASSIC AND COLLECTOR CARS

When vehicles are a passion, there is no detail too small when crafting the right protection. While the same basics apply for liability, the details in the policy language matter with custom, classic, and collector vehicles. The values are sometimes hard to determine due to specialty repairs and the cost of aftermarket parts, as well as the use of such vehicles in parades that may be excluded in standard auto policies.

Custom or modified vehicles are ones that have functional upgrades, improved performance, or unique body work. Custom-built cars can be as complex as custom design of all features from the paint job to door handles to interior features. Or they may have just a few upgrades like rims, brush guards, or a travel rack. These are items that need to be discussed with your advisor to ensure you have the right coverage in place.

Hidden Risks:

- If you lift your vehicle, make sure you discuss what size lift kit is on the vehicle as there are restrictions on the personal auto policy with how high they can be lifted.

- There is typically limited to no coverage for customization, so be sure to endorse the correct coverage limit based on upgrades made to the vehicle.

The words "Collector" or "Classic" car are interchangeable terms when insuring vehicles. Collector is the broader term and includes newer exotic vehicles along with classic vehicles. Classic vehicles typically date from early 1900 to around 1980. Some collectors break it down further to vintage or antique vehicles, but they should all be insured with the same considerations and *not* on a standard personal auto policy unless altered with the correct endorsements like agreed value and custom equipment.

When repairing or replacing a custom vehicle after a loss, the policy language really matters. As we discussed earlier in this chapter, OEM parts, agreed value, choice of repair shops, and general flexibility at time of claim is very important when it comes to putting your passion piece back together.

If you decide to **ship your vehicle** instead of driving it, consider some of these risk mitigation options:

- Ship in an enclosed transport versus open trailer.

- Do your research and get a few different bids.

    - Hire a reputable and honest transportation company (do not just choose one from an online search). Dishonest transportation companies are out there and are an easy way for thieves to steal your vehicle or personal belongings.

    - Verify the transportation company's registration.

- Find out whether the transportation company is a broker or carrier.

    Ascertain whether the vehicle will stay with the same driver/transportation company or if there are portions of the transportation subbed out to other contractors.

- Keep the vehicle registrations with you.

- Don't store personal belongings in vehicles that are being shipped. Most auto policies do not provide coverage for personal belongings, so if they are damaged, stolen, or lost while in transit, there would be limited to no coverage on your auto policy for the loss.

- Consider how the vehicle is being covered for physical loss while being hauled. Does the driver have insurance that covers damage to your vehicle, or would you have to file a claim on your own auto insurance if damaged while hauling?

- Make sure to have a pre- and post-delivery inspection.

- If shipping overseas, consider additional factors such as containerized shipping versus the roll-on/roll-off method. Investigate what additional coverage may be required for events such as flood damage, pirate attacks, or the vehicle falling overboard.

Hidden Risk: If a vehicle shipment does end up in the water, how it got there is very important to determine whether coverage was in place or not.

  - Flotsam: when items accidentally fall into the water, sometimes due to a storm or ship wrecking.

  - Jetsam: when a vessel must throw a container overboard due to any emergency. This is where we see a lot of gaps in coverage come into play. Since the act is intentional, most insurance policies would decline coverage if the vehicle were damaged due to jetsam.

OTHER WHEELS IN YOUR LIFE

Outside of your standard vehicle, there may be other wheels in your life such as golf carts, mopeds, electric scooters, and ATVs that fall outside the appetite of the standard auto policy but should be covered on a recreational vehicle policy. Typically, for coverage to exist, the vehicle(s) needs to be listed on the policy. The only time this does not apply is if the vehicle is used to maintain the property (for example, a riding lawnmower). However, if you lend your riding lawnmower to your neighbor, there could be gaps in your coverage because coverage is usually provided on insured premises.

Common wheels outside of cars:

- **Four-Wheelers/ATVs:** While they are a lot of fun and can be extremely useful, they are dangerous and create a large liability exposure. Often people assume four-wheelers and ATVs are covered on the homeowners policy, which is not always the case. If there is coverage, it is typically limited to when the vehicle is on premises. The moment the vehicle leaves the insured's premises, liability coverage stops.

- **Golf Carts:** These have the same considerations as ATVs, especially if you are using them on-road. You need to obtain a golf cart policy that provides liability coverage while on the road and add full coverage if you are concerned with things like theft.

- **Motorcycles:** Most people get liability coverage on motorcycles for legal purposes, but they underestimate the need for uninsured/ underinsured (UM/UIM) coverage while riding. Typically, if a motorcyclist is injured while riding, the injuries are severe and medical bills add up quickly. We've all seen the roadside reminders to keep an eye out for riders. What if you are that unfortunate rider who is hit and the driver irresponsibly takes off (which happens in a lot of cases, unfortunately)? UM/UIM is the coverage that will pay out to you and your family to try and make you whole again. These limits cannot exceed your base bodily injury liability, so it's important to "buy up" the base liability so you can get the proper UM/UIM.

  Example: Let's say you want to purchase $100,000 per person / $300,000 per accident limits for your liability in case you hurt someone else or damage their property. This is the max you can purchase in uninsured/underinsured motorist coverage as well. Consider increasing the base bodily injury limits to the max available like $500,000 per accident or $250,000 per person / $500,000 per person limits. That way, you can purchase the same limits in UM/UIM to protect yourself.

If you ride a **dirt bike** on major roads, you will also want to consider coverage similar to your standard motorcycle.

Bicycles seem simple and straightforward. Depending on how you use them, you may need to assess whether coverage in your homeowners policy will apply or if a separate policy is needed. Typically, activities like racing are excluded, so if your bicycle is stolen at a race you are participating in, the homeowners personal property coverage would not extend, and liability is excluded.

In discussions of bicycles, we cannot forget **electric bikes**. Unlike your typical bike, an e-bike has a little more go and should be added to some sort of liability policy while on the road.

Mopeds are a gray area when it comes to licensing but *not* insurance. If you own a moped, you need insurance even if the moped is not licensed. As a driver of the moped, you still have liability exposure if you damage someone's property or injure them while operating your moped. For coverage to be in place, it needs to be added to your auto policy or a recreational vehicle policy of some sort with a minimum of liability. If you are worried about your moped being stolen or damaged due to an accident, you will want to make sure to include full coverage with comprehensive and collision deductibles to be able to use insurance to cover the cost to replace or repair.

HOW TO HELP WITH AUTO RATES

If you want the most individualized premium for your auto insurance, then you need to participate in a telematics program, which is offered through most insurance companies. Every company has a different name for them, but they all do the same thing. They collect personal driving data such as speed, time of day you drive, hard braking, and other factors to determine if you are a "safer" driver than the public. Along with the different names, companies have different parameters around the programs they offer—from length of time you need to participate in the tracking, who must participate (all household members, only kids, etc.), and what is being taken into consideration for the driving data being collected.

- **Consider this:** If you are thinking, "I don't want big brother tracking me," but you have a vehicle with technology (built-in navigation, OnStar), then you are already being "tracked." So, why not save some money on your auto for this?

- **Consider this:** If you are a parent and track your child via their phone, the telematics programs offered by insurance companies can do the same and send you alerts about location, speed, and other useful information while your child is learning to drive.

Accidents happen and that is why you carry insurance, but not all accidents require insurance to get involved if the party at fault can handle the damage out of pocket.

Like homeowners, auto accidents are typically chargeable for 3 to 5 years. While any unexpected expenses are not ideal, sometimes paying out of pocket is the better choice as the surcharge for the auto claim over 3 to 5 years may end up costing you more than paying it out of pocket.

Example: You are driving to work, and while sitting in traffic, you sneeze. As your eyes open back up, you notice brake lights in front of you and slam on your brakes. Unfortunately, you nudge the car in front of you, only causing damage to their bumper. Since no one is injured, you exchange auto insurance information and agree to call each other later in the day. When you reach out to the other person, they mention they've already received an estimate for the bumper, which is $1,700 on their 10-year-old sedan. Based on that information, you feel you could potentially pay out of pocket for the repairs. While surcharges for claims range drastically, if this is your first accident, a 15% increase for the first year is what I use as a general starting point. In this example, you currently pay $3,900 a year for auto insurance. If you file this claim, you can expect to see a surcharge for 3 to 5 years.

Equation: $3,900 (annual auto cost) x 0.15 (surcharge) = $585 x 3 (years) = $1,755.

That's more than the claim cost. If the claim is charged for 5 years, you will pay even more than that. What happens if you are in a second accident during that period? You will see a large increase in cost and potentially become un-insurable based on loss history.

*Note: If there are injuries, **always** get insurance involved ASAP.*

I don't share this with you to make you hate insurance. My goal is for you to use it to your advantage and understand when it is beneficial as a consumer to file a claim and use your auto insurance.

While all the technology in vehicles is useful and often fun, it comes with higher repair bills when a vehicle is damaged. Consider a vehicle's bumper. It used to just be a piece of metal to guard the body of the vehicle from damage if it was bumped and was typically easy to fix. Today's bumper's purpose has changed. It now acts as a tool to help guide the driver to back up easier and let them know when they are too close to an object. And with those technology enhancements has come not only an increased cost of the bumper itself, but also the labor required to install a bumper with "bells and whistles" costs more. While bells and whistles are nice, consider the additional cost it may add to your insurance for repair or replacement of these items.

Bold young drivers can really hurt your pocketbook when you add them to your auto insurance. And while you have a great kid, they are learning a new skill (driving a powerful machine). Some ways to help with rates for a young driver include:

- Good student discount: Typically a 3.0 GPA is needed to qualify. This discount really helps young driver rates. Be sure to let your advisor know if your child's GPA will help them qualify for a discount.

- Some companies provide credits if the new driver participates in driver's education.

- If you are getting your child their own vehicle, consider one that does not need a loan so that you need only carry liability. The cost for full coverage on a vehicle with a young driver can sometimes double or triple the cost, depending on the vehicle.

- When children go away to school over 100 miles and leave a vehicle at home, make sure to let your advisor know. You will receive a credit since they will be designated as a limited-use driver due to the fact that they will be using the vehicle(s) a lot less than when they lived at home.

When building your auto insurance program, focus on the right liability and deductible limits for you. If there is still room in your budget for the bells and whistles like new car replacement, accident forgiveness, and other endorsements, then consider adding those. Do *not*, however, lower your liability so that you can add new car replacement to a policy and stay in your "budget." The additional cost for this "added" benefit does not outweigh the gap you've created in your larger financial protection, which is the most important piece of your coverage picture.

Chapter 4:
Personal Excess Liability

While every person's life has liability, few people pay attention to it when discussing their insurance program. And yet it is the most important and affordable part of insurance.

Liability insurance benefits range from defense cost coverage should someone sue you due to your negligence to paying out for the judgment or settlement. Your liability coverage should *not* be less than your **net worth** and should take future income and assets into account. If an insurance agent tells you they cannot get you the limit necessary, you most likely have outgrown that agent. A few companies offer $50,000,000+ in coverage when needed with straightforward underwriting. Working with the right insurance advisor is key to being able to access the right markets and guidance available at time of purchase.

Tip: Underwriting has become stricter on large increases to umbrella limits, so it is important to buy the right limit now and steadily increase it as needed. Sometimes it can be hard to go from a $5 million to $20 million umbrella without an explanation such as a business sale or purchase. Otherwise, a good underwriter will work with a client over time to increase coverage to the appropriate level as they become more familiar and comfortable with the account as a whole.

Did you know? You can "stack" liability policies in order to purchase the correct amount needed for your lifestyle. There are specific conditions that each "layer" must meet before the next "layer" kicks in. You cannot just buy different umbrellas from carriers and assume they will stack on top of each other. Stacking is something that needs to be outlined prior to issuing multiple umbrella policies. If not, only one could end up responding based on policy language.

Your lifestyle choices are what make up your liability exposure. From the home or homes you own and their characteristics (pools, playgrounds, etc.) to your cars and toys (ATVs, golf carts, etc.) to how you live your life (owning pets, driving fast, owning a big boat with large engines, flying your drone)—all these choices increase your liability and risk exposure. Liability is present even when you're doing simple activities such as hosting a gathering at your home, giving a kid's birthday party, or barbecuing with friends on Friday night. When you own a home, vehicle, watercraft, or other "fun things," understand the dangers and possible exposure to losing a lot should someone get hurt or things go awry.

There is no way to predict who is going to be injured because of your negligence or how badly they will be hurt. Liability can stem from a variety of circumstances—from being found at fault for a multicar pileup to someone being injured playing on your playground in the backyard. With everything you do and every choice you make, there is an associated risk. Sometimes that risk can also include liability.

There are a few forms of liability such as medical payments, personal liability, and excess liability. We've explored these topics in previous chapters. We're doing so again because liability coverage is *very* important as it protects your most valuable assets and provides the defense cost should you need it during a claim.

Typically, with personal liability, the defense cost is "outside the limit of liability." There are situations, however, where defense cost is "inside the limit of liability," which we usually see in the non-admitted markets but could be in some standard forms.

Example:

- **Outside the limit:** If you have $500,000 in homeowners' liability with a $2 million umbrella and are sued for $2.5 million, the insurance company will fight on your behalf, if necessary, to settle for the right amount. Should the final settlement be $2.5 million, your two policies would pay out that full amount, regardless of what the insurance company paid in defense cost.

- **Inside the limit:** This means that whatever the insurance company spends on defense will be subtracted from the liability limit within the policy. So, for the above example, if the insurance company spent $400,000 in defense, they would only cover a judgment or settlement of up to $2.1 million.

A typical objection to high umbrella limits is "The higher limit puts a bigger target on my back for a larger claim." While that seems logical, the truth is you already have a target on your back with the assets you possess. The more assets (tangible and intangible), the bigger the target. Those assets will be discovered at time of a loss when your insurance is exhausted and the other party still has unpaid damages or judgment. By carrying the right liability limit for your current and future assets, the insurance company will defend on your behalf and will fight for you (since the check is coming out of their account at the end of the day).

Hidden Risk: It is important that your insurance advisor and attorney talk to ensure all entities in which you are personally involved are properly covered and listed on your insurance documents. If they are not, there is no coverage.

It is also important when titling and structuring assets to understand how those entities need to operate to prevent piercing the structure's veil. For example, if you set up an LLC for rentals but use your personal credit card to pay the bills or collect rent in your personal name, that entity could be seen as a "shell," and a good attorney will find a way to go after the entities and your personal assets. The ecosystem between your insurance protection, estate-planning documents including titling of assets, and wealth-building are all intertwined and must be looked at as one when discussing liability needs.

You may be thinking, "I live a simple life. I don't need too much liability insurance." This is another reason liability coverage is so important. For example, you cause a bad car accident and the state minimum coverage you purchased was not enough, now causing you to have your wages garnished to pay restitution to the other party. Investing a little more in the right insurance up front can allow you to maintain the life you have. Here are a few of the common, everyday hidden risks to consider:

- While animals can be the apple of our eye, insurance companies see them as a liability and a big part of underwriting. Factors to consider: the breed of dog you own, the number of horses (or other farm animals) owned, or whether the animal is considered exotic, like a ball python. Whatever pulls at your heart could leave you vulnerable at a time of a loss if not disclosed up front because some policies include exclusions relating to animals.

- Are you the hostess with the mostest? While hosting parties is fun, it also comes with responsibilities. Consider purchasing a special events policy for events like fundraising activities (political, schools, organizations you are involved in) that will be hosted at your home. Or maybe a large celebration like a graduation party, milestone birthdays, and other occasions where there may be an unusually large number of people on the property or the event could be seen as outside "personal use." In addition, consider hiring a bartending company to serve your guest drinks and maybe a chef to cook. Serving liquor to your guests can sometimes become a gray area should a loss occur once they leave your home after drinking too much.

- Backyard attractions make for fun diversions, but insurance companies view playsets, trampolines, pools, and ziplines as an attractive nuisance that increases your exposure for loss. With that comes exclusions within a policy. Make sure to discuss these items both inside and outside your home with your insurance advisor.

- What is your commute to work like? The longer your commute to and from work, the higher your possibility of causing an accident. Maybe you drive a lot of back roads or highways. Understanding how and where you use your vehicle is important when understanding your liability risk.

- Giving back is a great contribution for both you and your community. However, activities like hosting events, sitting on a nonprofit board, and other community engagements can increase your liability exposure as well as a company's willingness to do business with you.

- When upgrading your home, it is important to make sure whoever is doing the work carries their own workers' compensation and general liability insurance as your personal homeowners and umbrella coverage may exclude liability for anyone working on premises.

- Occupation matters with liability underwriting, and sometimes if an individual or family has a higher-profile occupation, it can cause companies to limit terms or add additional exclusions to the policy to limit their exposure and feel comfortable offering some form of terms for coverage.

Examples: A politician, high-profile doctor, attorney, or social media influencer. Sometimes with these occupations, we will see insurance companies add exclusions, for example, Libel and Slander, on the personal lines coverage. It is recommended to look to a commercial policy to try to cover exposures typically covered in a personal policy but may now be excluded based on your specific profession.

What you have on the premises and do day-to-day can change a company's appetite for wanting to do business. It is important to explain all aspects to an advisor, either at the start of the policy or throughout the years as you make changes to your living situation.

The terms that are used for different types of liability insurance coverage vary depending on if it is auto, homeowners, rental property, etc. It is critical to understand the different types.

- **Medical Payments**

  - On homeowners: This is a no-fault coverage and pays out to guests who are injured on your premises. Typically, medical payments are used to help pay for smaller injuries and help lower the likelihood that the individual will sue you.

  - On auto insurance: This coverage can be used for you as well as members of your household. This is a no-fault coverage and intended to be used for medical deductibles and copays after a loss occurs—regardless of if you or another party are at fault for the loss.

- **Personal Injury Protection:** An upgraded version of medical payments, this coverage is only offered in specific states. It includes everything medical payments does plus funeral expenses, work loss, survivors' loss, and payments for essential services.

- **Premises Liability:** It is important to understand what type of liability you are purchasing when you buy homeowners or rental property coverage. If the liability policy is premises liability, it will typically only cover the owners' negligence for injuries arising out of failure to maintain that specific property.

- **Personal Liability:** This is a broader form of liability policy that can be added to a homeowners policy and would cover your negligence on your premises as well as if you are found negligent off your premises for bodily injuries or property damages to others.

- **Worldwide Liability:** With worldwide liability, you have liability coverage anywhere in the world. Standard companies will limit liability to the United States and its territories. Affluent insurance companies (i.e., Chubb, PURE, Cincinnati, AIG) will provide coverage for you when you're in other countries. If you travel often, worldwide liability is a must!

- **First Dollar Coverage:** Typically found on an umbrella policy within the personal insurance space, first dollar coverage kicks in as soon as the event occurs, and no deductible or underlying coverage is needed. This is not standard and usually an enhancement within certain insurance companies' policies.

Consider this when choosing the liability limit: If you do not have enough liability coverage for the damage you cause, the courts will find a way to make you pay. Whether it's through wage garnishment of future earnings, liquidity in your home, or other assets, the courts can make sure the other party is made whole again due to your negligence.

Risk management is the "umbrella" category that encompasses everything related to potential liability exposure. To protect your assets, you work with an attorney to create a trust and will to make sure you title different assets properly. You will most likely work with a financial advisor to make sure all your hard-earned money is working hard for you. And you work with a risk manager to make sure if you do find yourself causing a bad loss, you have the right protection to allow you to maintain your lifestyle.

A liability umbrella provides a great deal of coverage. For basics, back in the auto chapter, there was the example of the auto accident on a rainy day. Let's say the individual had $600,000 in medical bills/lost wages, and now the $500,000 combined single limit is no longer enough. Your umbrella would kick in then and start to provide coverage.

UMBRELLA VERSUS EXCESS LIABILITY POLICY

Umbrella and **Excess Liability** are often used interchangeably within marketing. However, the actual policy language illustrates that these are very different policies.

Excess liability is just that—in excess of the underlying liability you have on your home, auto, watercraft, etc. The excess liability coverage follows what is in the underlying policy, meaning whatever exclusions apply there also apply within this policy. For coverage to apply at time of loss, the asset must be listed on the excess policy with underlying coverage in place.

Umbrella liability is broader and can provide the first dollar coverage if an exclusion that was on an underlying policy does not appear in the umbrella policy.

This brings us to another important piece in umbrella coverage—the underlying liability requirements on the home, auto, watercraft, etc., policies. These requirements are outlined within the policy; however, most people do not pay attention to these potential gaps in coverage. Typically, we see minimum limit requirements on underlying policies similar to the following:

- Homeowners: $300,000 in liability coverage
- Auto/Watercrafts/Recreational Vehicle Insurance: $250,000 per person / $500,000 per accident / $100,000 in property damage OR $300,000 combined single limits liability coverage

Note: These limits are set by the companies and do vary. Read your specific policy language to confirm that no gaps exist.

Hidden Risk: A gap in coverage can be a huge problem. If a client only has $100,000 in liability on a rental property and the umbrella requires $300,000 in underlying liability before coverage kicks in, the client would be responsible for that difference of $200,000. This is one reason why having all your coverages with one insurance advisor is important to make sure these "simple" gaps do not occur.

Like the home and auto policies, the excess liability policies can also be endorsed to include broader coverage based on a client's specific need.

- **Uninsured/Underinsured Coverage:** DON'T get this confused with uninsured/underinsured **motorist** coverage. It is very different and applies to you and your family outside an automobile. This coverage is often overlooked but very useful. Who asks their friends what their liability limits are when going over to their home? Or maybe a restaurant doesn't have the right coverage. The situations in which you or a household member could be injured and where that person or business is inadequately covered are endless. Of course, you could sue the responsible party, but do you really want to go through years of attorneys and time spent jumping through hoops to get pennies on the dollar? This is a unique coverage that is not available from many standard companies and would provide coverage to help your family with medical bills, loss of wages, and potential changes in lifestyle.

- **Directors and Officers (D&O):** Giving back to your community and helping with nonprofit organizations can be rewarding. But what happens when the board is accused of a misleading statement, neglect, or misusing funds? When you sit on a nonprofit board, the decisions you make can and will be held against you at time of a loss. If the loss exceeds the limits of the D&O coverage that is in place for the organization, then your personal assets are vulnerable.

    - **Hidden Risk:** How D&O works: While most legitimate organizations have at least $1 million in coverage, that does not go as far as one would think because the cost of defense and judgment are paid out of the same limit (known as "inside the limit of liability"). If five people sit on a board, the cost to defend those five board members can add up quickly and exhaust the limit before a settlement is even declared. If the policy limits are exhausted before all damages are paid, then the board members' assets are potentially vulnerable to make the injured party whole.

    - **Example:** Any nonprofit board you sit on presents an exposure, even a neighborhood board. There is a local parade that my neighborhood puts on every year. It is well known in the area and can draw upwards of 50,000 people to celebrate St. Patrick's Day. I sat on this board for a while, and we oversaw planning all logistics for the day, from street closure, security, parade route, and more. With that responsibility grows liability exposure.

What would have happened if someone had been injured at this event? Or, even worse, if multiple people had gotten hurt and our organization's limits were exhausted? My personal assets could have been vulnerable. Even if a claim is frivolous, defense coverage is still needed. While this is a large-scale event, people can still be injured at small block parties or accused of funds being misused to "upgrade" the neighborhood.

- **Employer's Liability:** When people work on your premises, your liability exposure increases dramatically. This coverage can help provide protection should an employee claim sexual harassment, discrimination, or wrongful termination while in the course of employment.

- **Uninsured/Underinsured Motorist Coverage:** When it comes to useful coverages, this one is at the top of the list. Not only because the number of uninsured and underinsured drivers is climbing, but also because this is the limit that protects your loved ones. What happens if you find yourself in an auto accident with someone who has no insurance or not enough insurance and you or multiple family members are severely injured? You can purchase an extra layer of protection on your umbrella policy to pay out in addition to the underlying coverage on your auto policy.

As previously mentioned, this coverage applies beyond vehicular circumstances. It can potentially provide protection for you and household members while a pedestrian or bicyclist. This is *not* automatically part of umbrella policies and must be added as an endorsement.

Policy language comes into play at time of uninsured/underinsured claims, and it's important that your adult children are not being carried on your auto or umbrella policy unless they live in your household as these coverages may not apply at time of loss.

BENEFITS OF HIGH-END INSURANCE COMPANIES

If you want flexibility in your excess liability coverage, the companies that are built to insure successful individuals and families include coverages that cater to lifestyle needs, including:

- **Supplemental Defense** includes some reimbursement for you to have a law firm of your choice to participate in your defense.

- **Crisis Management:** In today's connected world, news travels fast. One might argue that the most important thing an individual can possess is a good reputation. What happens when that is in jeopardy? Liability coverage can be added and allows for reimbursement of a crisis management or PR firm.

- **Family Protection** provides coverage for the unthinkable, such as stalking threats, hijacking, wrongful taking or detention of child, cyberbullying, and more. It provides monetary reimbursement for lost wages along with supportive services such as psychiatric care, temporary relocation, and increased security.

- **Watercraft Rental** can provide liability for watercrafts rented or chartered, typically up to 30 days. Size restrictions for vessels could apply.

- **Aircraft Rental** applies when you are renting or chartering an aircraft for less than 30 days and you or a resident of the household is *not* the pilot.

Regarding liability, it is important to remember that defense is still needed even in the instances of a frivolous lawsuit. With the proper liability limits, the insurance company can pay for your defense along with potential damages up to policy limits. However, once the insurance limits are exhausted, the insurance company no longer has a duty to defend, leaving you on the hook for your defense cost.

When designing your insurance program, it's best to take into account what you do, the assets you currently hold and will have, and how everything in your lifestyle drives your specific liability coverage needs.

With the right liability limit, you can enjoy your lifestyle knowing you have the right protection in place should something go wrong. Do *not* be afraid to talk to your advisor and consider them a "board" member to your life. They can help guide and protect you as you build and maintain wealth.

Chapter 5:
Insuring Your Collections

If everyone could be lucky enough to have something they are passionate about, the world would be a better place. Just as passions add value to life, insuring them on a collectibles policy adds valuable protection for those items. Collectible policies have a lot of different names in the industry, with all offering relatively similar coverages. You may also hear these policies called a valuable articles policy, floater, inland marine coverage, or they can be added to a homeowners policy as a rider or endorsement.

So, why do you need to insure items like jewelry, art, sports memorabilia, hunting trophies, and other valuables on a separate policy?

Most homeowners policies have sub-limits for "collectible" types of items such as jewelry, art, furs, coins, wine, and more.

The *standard ISO form HO-3 (01-00)* policy has the below internal limits for 10-plus items such as:

A. $200 on money, bank notes, bullion, gold other than goldware, silver other than silverware, platinum other than platinum ware, coins, medals, scrips, stored value cards, and smart cards.

B. $1,500 on securities, accounts, deeds, evidence of debt, letter of credit, notes other than bank notes, manuscripts, personal records, passports, tickets, and stamps. This limit applies to these categories regardless of medium (paper or computer software) on which such material exist. This limit includes cost to research, replace, or restore the information from the lost or damaged material.

C. $1,500 on watercrafts of all types, including their trailers, furnishings, equipment, and outboard engines or motors.

D. $1,500 on trailers or semitrailers not used with watercrafts of all types.

E. $1,500 for loss by theft of jewelry, watches, furs, precious and semiprecious stones. Loose stones are usually not covered within any type of coverage. It is important to talk with your advisor if you do have a loose stone to make sure you purchase the proper coverage.

F. $2,500 for loss by theft of firearms and related equipment.

G. $2,500 for loss by theft of silverware, silverplated ware, gold ware, gold-plated ware, platinum ware, platinum-plated ware, and pewter ware. This includes flatware, hollowware, tea sets, trays, and trophies made of or including silver, gold, or pewter.

H. $2,500 on property, on the "residence premises" used primarily for "business" purposes.

I. $500 on property, away from the "residence premises," used primarily for "business" purposes. However, this limit does not apply to loss of electronic apparatus like computers and other property described in categories J and K below.

J. $1,500 on electronic apparatus and accessories, while in or upon a "motor vehicle" but only if the apparatus is equipped to be operated by power from the "motor vehicle's" electrical system while still capable of being operated by other power sources. Accessories include antennae, tapes, wires, records, discs, or other media that can be used with any apparatus described in this Category J.

K. $1,500 on electronic apparatus and accessories used primarily for "business," while away from the "residence premises" and not in or upon a "motor vehicle." The apparatus must be equipped to be operated by power from the "motor vehicle's" electrical system while still capable of being operated by other power sources. Accessories include antennae, tapes, wires, records, discs, or other media that can be used with any apparatus described in this Category K.

These limits are the **max you will get paid**, *not* per item; also, the homeowners deductible applies at time of loss.

Every company can adjust the policy language to include or remove sub-limits as well as the dollar amount associated with the categories listed above. It is important to read your specific policy to understand what limitations may be within your policies.

When insuring collectibles, there are two limit categories in which you can insure the items—blanket limit or schedule limit.

- **Blanket Limit:** This coverage option requires the insured to come up with a single value for the entire collection (jewelry, art, sports memorabilia, etc.) and then add a max per-item limit.

    - It is important that the max per-item limit covers the most expensive item in your collection.

    - When there are outliers in value within those collection categories, consider scheduling those specific items.

- This tends to be the easiest way to insure collectibles as it does not require the client to come up with an inventory with specific dollar amounts to get the coverage. You will need documentation at time of claim, so it's important to have some type of record for these items should a loss occur.

- It is a cost-effective way to insure your valuable items.

  Each category has a different per $100 or $1,000 cost associated with it, so it is important to look at insuring all your collections and not assume the jewelry rate (which tends to be the highest) is what it would cost to insure items like art (which tends to be one of the cheaper categories to protect).

- **Schedule Limit:** This coverage option is when the insured lists the specific item, with description and dollar amount for that item.

  - Consider this option for higher-value or rare items.

  - This is the best way to protect items that are used on a consistent basis that have a higher likelihood of experiencing a loss. Examples include items like wedding bands, watches, and some other specialty items.

There are three main reasons to have a collections policy:

1. **Agreed Value:** This is beneficial as the client and the insurance company agree at the start of the policy on a value for a specific item. This allows the client to know up front if there is a loss that the insurance company would be willing to pay to repair or replace that item.

   This is unlike with some homeowners policies where property is covered on an actual cash value basis, which takes depreciation into account at time of loss.

2. **No Deductible:** On a true collection policy, there is no deductible that applies at time of loss. This means your item(s) are repaired or replaced without any out-of-pocket expense.

    There can sometimes be deductibles added to policies for numerous reasons, including standard policy for that company, loss history, or insured's choice to help offset some of the cost to insure the collection.

3. **Broader policy language** for coverage and how claims are handled:

    – Coverage for things like diminished value, which can occur after a loss to a collectible that has been repaired: The value after the repair is not always the same as before damage occurred, in which case the insurance company will pay for the difference in value on that item.

    – When your collection involves sets and pairs, it's important to have the flexibility to choose what you want to do with the undamaged piece(s) if the other piece(s) are beyond repair. Some carriers can turn the undamaged piece(s) in to get full replacement value verses only being reimbursed for the damaged piece(s).

Depending on how and where you collect, sometimes looking at higher-end and specialty insurance companies to insure your collection is necessary as they include additional coverages such as:

- **Additional Replacement Cost on your items:** Usually around 150%. In today's crazy market, having agreed value on your collection is not enough as one day a bottle of whiskey or piece of art could be worth $100,000 and the next day worth $150,000 because of a market change. If you experience a loss at the height of a market shift and do not have this coverage, you will find yourself with a financial loss and potentially unable to replace the damaged item at that time.

- **Automatic Coverage for new items:** The time frame ranges on how long the automatic coverage is, but it's usually around 30 days and usually applies to categories with existing coverage. This is extremely important if you are an avid collector and like to gather new items as you travel or buy on a frequent basis. This additional coverage gives you the peace of mind to know that as you grow your collection, you have coverage.

- **Worldwide Coverage:** Some people may assume they have this coverage, but that is not always the case, and having your collection covered anywhere can be important based on the way one lives. Whether you travel with your jewelry, purchase new wine or spirits and art while you are traveling, or have hunting trophies, knowing you have coverage for your items anywhere in the world can give you the assurance to grow and display your collection with confidence.

- **Equipment Breakdown:** This coverage is important coverage if you have collections that are sensitive to temperature or humidity change. Typically, we see this need with collectors of wine and spirits as well as art and hunting trophies.

- **Collection Services:** This enhances your collecting experience from collection management, appraisal services, and risk management to help with some of the risks that come along with collecting, as discussed in this chapter.

It is important to keep documentation of the items that are included in your collection, which should include photo(s), description(s), and value(s). Even if documentation is not required to issue coverage, it will be required at time of a claim. Typically, you should have values reevaluated every few years or as the market changes.

If you see your collectibles as assets, it is even more important to have the right insurance. Whether it is for the art you collect (physical or NFT), the wine and whiskey you enjoy, couture clothing with handbags, or sports memorabilia and hunting trophies, to have full protection for these assets and be able to replace the item or receive monetary value, they will need to be insured for the appropriate limit. That is accomplished by a collections policy.

Vehicles can also fall onto this type of policy depending on the type of auto collection you have.

When it comes to protecting your collections, it is not just about the monetary protection that one needs to consider, but also how the collection is used, displayed, and stored.

How the collection items are used may seem straightforward, but it is surprising how often that is not the case. For example, if you keep art or jewelry outside the home, it is important to let the insurance company know, especially if the item is on consignment in a business, museum, or personal residence as there can be exclusions within policies for this type of use. Remember, these are personal policies; if you see your collections as a business, you can obtain coverage in the commercial market for better protection.

Indications that your collection may be more of a "business" verses personal use include:

- If you find yourself selling or trading your items on a frequent basis, you could be seen as a broker or dealer of those items.

- You allow others to rent items from your collection (clothing, art, jewelry, etc.)

Who has physical possession of the item also matters, especially as we go through wealth transfer and assets, such as collections, start to get passed to the next generation. It is important that the person(s) receiving the item(s) obtains coverage for the valuables and does not rely on the individual who gave them the item to continue carrying the coverage as policy coverage does not transfer with ownership.

Another decision when it comes to collections is how to display and appreciate the items one collects. It is not just as simple as putting a nail in the wall to hang art or a shelf in the study to display whiskey alongside your coin collection. To make sure you can enjoy your collection for a long time, hire a professional to hang or construct the display for your specific collection. The display isn't a place for you to cut corners on cost and hire the handyman down the road or accomplish a DIY project; spend the time and money on a professional installation team for your specific type of collection. Here are a few tips to keep in mind when looking to display your items:

- Make sure the item(s) are not in direct sunlight.

- Items should not be displayed on, near, or in direct contact with heating and cooling systems.

- Keeping rooms at consistent temperature and with humidity under control is critical to keeping pieces in top shape.

- Make sure when cleaning the collection, it is with the appropriate cleaning products and that the cleaning material is disposed of properly.

For items you do not want to display, you may feel like you are doing the right thing by placing those valuables in a place hard to see, like the top shelf of a closet or in the back of a dresser or under the mattress, but the truth is that provides a false sense of protection. Where your collection is kept when not in use should not be a decision taken lightly. When determining where to keep your items, consider:

- How often do you wear or use the item? If the answer is infrequently, consider storing the item(s) in an off-site secure facility such as a bank vault or storage facility that specializes in storing specific items. Do *not* keep valuables in a basic storage unit. Not only is it bad for your items, but also the elements such as temperature change and insects could be excluded coverages within the policy.

- How replaceable is the item? Is it something you can easily replace or is the item an heirloom that if damaged or lost would be irreplaceable? If the answer is irreplaceable based on market availability or emotional attachment, consider this when storing the item and choose a secure, climate-controlled space.

- Is your home regularly occupied and secured? If it is not regularly occupied, remember that when determining how many valuable assets you want to keep at this home. This is especially true if you answer no regarding your property not being secured. Having fire and burglar alarms can add a significant amount of protection to your valuables to help avoid or limit the amount of damage that could occur due to a loss. And just because you have a trusted person staying at your home or checking in doesn't mean your property is safe. Over 50% of home thefts occur by someone the homeowner knows (family member, friend, or household staff).

What happens when you do experience a loss to an item or items in your collection? The repair and replacement process can be very revealing of the terms of the insurance coverage one purchased. Do not wait for a claim to learn about the gaps in your collection's protection.

The list is unlimited when it comes to types of collections. That's why having a special policy for your collections that allows you to find an expert to help you repair or replace your item is imperative. While you may think that's included in the policy, that is not the case. Having the right resources to help repair and replace items is unique to luxury and specialty insurance companies.

Example: You have a dinner party, and as a guest is admiring your Andy Warhol painting, another guest bumps into them, causing their glass of red wine to coat the Warhol. Paintings such as a Warhol are not replaceable and ideally would be repaired by an artist who has studied Warhol and appreciates the craftsmanship and can restore the painting appropriately, which is an option you would have with the right coverage.

With the wrong insurance company or coverage, the painting may be deemed a total loss. You would be offered pennies on the dollar for the piece of art and not even given the option to repair. You would either have to pay for the damages out of pocket or expect the lowball offer and turn over your painting to the insurance company for the claim payment.

Traveling is another often overlooked area when it comes to protecting valuables. Even if the collection coverage does provide worldwide coverage, when you travel, especially abroad, flashy jewelry and couture items can make you a target for theft and other losses. One way to stay safe and protect your valuable items while traveling is to dress to blend in and consider wearing costume jewelry.

If you do intend to travel with some of your nicer items, make sure you consider some of the following:

- Keep valuable jewelry with you and do not include in checked-in luggage.

- If you are shipping items, make sure you use an insured service with tracking and experience in shipping your specific items.

    - It is also important to understand how the transit for the item will work. Is the entire shipment being conveyed via one provider or are there subcontractors along the route, and how does protection coverage apply as the item(s) change hands?

    - Does your insurance provide coverage while the item is being shipped? There are some conditions that need to be met prior to shipping, and if they are not, the insurance company can deny the claim.

- If you plan to be in a different country and stay in a hotel for a long time, consider getting a safety deposit box at a bank nearby to store your valuable items while you are not wearing or using them.

  Hotel safes are not as secure as one may think, and items are easily accessible to staff members.

As with every line of insurance coverage, it is important to remember the basis to insurance: to transfer the risk of replacing items you would not feel financially comfortable replacing and shift that risk to the insurance company in exchange for a premium. Sometimes with collectibles, they hold more of an emotional than monetary value and could never truly be replaced even if damaged or lost. In this case, it would not be necessary to include those items in a collections policy.

There is also an argument for self-insuring lower-value items in general and starting a savings account that you could rely on if you experience a loss to your collection(s) and would want to replace the items. As we've discussed in previous chapters, filing claims is the last-resort option as keeping your claims history clean will allow you to keep the right insurance. Remember, your personal insurance is an ecosystem, and too many claims on one policy could affect the rest.

What is considered a collectible is broad, and one should not assume that coverage exists within their homeowners policy or that there is no coverage available for their specific collection need. The market is changing daily, and the ability to consider insurance for protection of assets will continue to evolve over the years.

Chapter 6:
Lifestyle Choices

Life is what we make of it. There is no reason to hold back and not enjoy each day to the fullest. But did you know your lifestyle is the road map to your insurance planning?

The choices you make daily play the biggest role when designing an insurance program. Whether you spend most of your time at home, engage in hobbies, or spend your spare time exploring the outdoors, the way you live your life matters.

Did you know? Underwriters will now Google clients and look at consumers' online presence—social media, news articles, etc.—to get a better idea of a client before doing business? Review your internet image and consider engaging a professional to monitor your image on the web.

In this chapter, we will dive deeper into how and why your lifestyle is the driving force in designing a personal insurance program specific for you. No one lives life the same way, so the risks one is exposed to on a regular basis vary. Lifestyle exposure is where most consumers find out that the "box" solution they've been sold their entire life no longer works for them. When thinking about your life, consider the lifestyle choices discussed here.

PROFESSION

How you make your living matters and can affect the type of personal insurance you need and your eligibility with a company. We will discuss this further in Chapter 7, but it is important that you separate business from pleasure. Insurance policies do *not* cross over, and your personal insurance coverage typically excludes coverage for business-related claims.

Individuals whose occupations are considered high profile, whether in their community or to the masses, have a higher risk for losses like theft, liability lawsuits, harassment, and even kidnapping, which makes insurance companies cautious when engaging in business. Some professions that typically require additional underwriting are:

- Athletes
- C-suite executives
- Politicians
- A-list celebrities
- Social media influencers
- Business owners

These professions need additional underwriting to cover the additional risks that exist and the corresponding losses that may occur. Factors that are taken into consideration include length of time in the spotlight, past risky behaviors, and the overlap between personal life and work life. These factors may influence a carrier's decision to limit specific coverage or decline offering terms, potentially leaving you with limited or less desirable options for your personal insurance program.

When available, certain professionals may want to explore additional coverages such as crisis management, supplemental defense (which would provide a sub-limit for your personal attorney to be co-counsel to the appointed insurance defense team), family protection, and cyber.

Note: While it won't be your first thought if you are considering changing careers, it is your responsibility to talk with your advisor to make sure there are no changes that need to be made within your insurance program. From coverage limits to new exclusions that may apply, there is no detail too small.

Rental properties are a way many people make a living. However, insurance coverage can sometimes become a checkbox in the closing process and not considered as thoroughly as it should be based on the financial investment and the foreseeable risks. Most rental portfolios run lean in the first years, and profitability is key. But cutting corners on insurance can cost more than just the repairs to that property and lost rental income. Being frugal with insurance could derail your investment career. The cost could be more than financial because the time involved resolving a claim will cost time and energy you won't be able to spend elsewhere. It is important to make sure that if you plan to build your wealth using real estate that you understand the role insurance plays in your long-term success.

While your occupation might not make you a millionaire, that doesn't mean you can't be sued like one. Maybe your name isn't one that everyone knows, but the internet is a powerful tool. Depending on your profession and overall net worth, an attorney may agree to take on a case to come after you for injuries to their client. If your personal liability covers the damages in question, your defense cost will be covered by insurance. Otherwise, you could be out of pocket for the defense cost and final judgment amount. And how would you cover that unexpected expense, potentially exceeding a million dollars in damages? Do you have investments or equity in your home or wages that could be garnished? Hopefully you won't have to liquidate any physical assets and downgrade your lifestyle.

When you work extremely hard for the lifestyle you enjoy, it is important that one bad day doesn't change the course of those efforts. Make sure that as you grow in your personal and professional life that your insurance program grows with you.

EMPLOYING PERSONS AND ENTITIES IN YOUR HOME

Life is busy and sometimes support around the home is necessary. Do not assume that people who are working on your premises are covered by the liability coverage within your homeowners and umbrella coverage. The state in which the employee is working can determine if there is any type of workers' compensation in the homeowners policy that will apply. There are many benefits to purchasing workers' compensation, employer's liability, and employment practice liability insurance. Each serves its own purpose when an individual is acting as an employer by hiring others to work on their premises. Workers to whom such coverage can apply include a monthly cleaning team or more frequent help like the full-time nanny, in-home health care, chef, or house manager.

It's important to understand insurance coverage responsibility when hiring at-home help. If the individual will be working for you full-time and you're their only employer, the responsibility could fall on you. However, if they work for you and other clients, it is in their best interest to purchase their own coverage to be protected at all job sites (and adjust pricing to offset cost for insurance).

The three coverages to consider when protecting yourself as an employer are:

- **Workers' Compensation:** "A system of insurance that reimburses an employer for damages that must be paid to an employee for injury occurring in the course of employment." (Source: Merriam-Webster.com Dictionary)

- **Employer's Liability:** "A coverage that helps pay a business owner's costs related to a lawsuit resulting from an employee's work-related injury or illness. Without employer's liability insurance, you'd have to pay for these legal costs out of pocket, which can get very expensive. Typically, this coverage is part of a workers' compensation insurance policy. But in monopolistic states, business owners may have to purchase it separately." (Source: TheHartford.com)

- **Employment Practice Liability:** This coverage "helps protect your business from employment-related claims, like wrongful termination, discrimination, and harassment." (Source: TheHartford.com)

In addition to purchasing the right insurance protection, you can take some initial steps to help eliminate the chance of a loss when an individual is working in your home.

1. Complete background checks on your employees before hiring (a shockingly large statistic reveals the amount of theft that occurs by individuals working within your home). Check, if possible, to see if they've been in lawsuits with other employers.

2. Lock valuables in a safe or keep them in a bank vault. Do not keep them in the open, in the top drawer of the dresser, or under the bed.

3. Do not talk about the type of items or amount of assets you own. It could make you a bigger target for frivolous lawsuits. Word could spread from your work to people you don't know, making you a target for burglary or a scam including a false lawsuit.

4. It is important to be kind and respectful to the individuals working on your premises. It is easy to let walls down and make comments in the moment that come off wrong or hurtful in a way and create the grounds for a discrimination or similar claim against you.

5. Create a checklist that includes steps for hiring and firing employees. Actions must remain consistent and documented. Sometimes these checklists can be provided by your insurance advisors.

There are additional concerns to consider relating to people working in your home daily.

First and foremost, references and background checks are a must. It's important to understand the job description, how and when the employee will interact with the family, whether travel is expected, and hiring and firing processes, along with who will pay that individual. All matter when designing this piece of the program.

Questions to consider regarding employees hired include:

- **Nanny:** Will your kids ride in the car? Will the nanny live with you? Who will pay the nanny (parents, grandparents, LLC)? These are just a few questions to explore with your advisors.

- **Chef:** It's often said that the way to one's heart is through the stomach. A chef can be a valuable team member in day-to-day life, especially when they cook for children whose palates change by the hour. In addition to the above considerations, it is important to consider the exposure a chef brings and what type of coverages you may want the chef to provide:

  - Coverage in case you or your children get severely sick by food

  - Coverage in case the chef damages your home in the course of their work

- **House Managers:** With the access a house manager has to you and your children's personal information, it's critical to perform a background check before making this hire. It is also important that they are a good steward of all information, including not disclosing your personal whereabouts (such as travel or kids' activities) and ensuring they use secure forms of communication when discussing sensitive information like finances. Consider having checks and balances in place to make sure one person does not have too much access that could allow for abuse of access and authority.

- **Medical Support:** It is also important to consider risks related to medical help in your home. In general, don't assume because you go through an agency to hire an individual that they have insurance (or have been properly vetted). Sometimes, the individuals working in your home are 1099 subcontractors and are not covered by the organization's insurance since they are not W2 employees. This means the responsibility and cost of obtaining coverage for damage to your home or injury to your family member is the responsibility of each subcontractor, who may or may not have coverage. If they do not have coverage, that responsibility and risk of loss falls back on you. Again, this could include damages if they are injured during the course of this employment. Just like with all other household employees, it's important to have processes for how hiring and firing is handled along with clear requests and requirements for the insurance that must be in place and who is responsible for obtaining and maintaining that coverage.

CYBER VULNERABILITIES

In today's world, it is not a matter of whether you will experience a cyberattack but when. Most individuals have a larger target on their back for personal cybercrime than small businesses because they lack the cybersecurity necessary to protect their personal data, which makes them easier targets with similar financial gain for the cybercriminal.

Everything in life is connected when you think about it. It starts with your phone, then maybe a watch, your car, and then your home. Possibly you have technology that is connected to other people in your personal ecosystem (parents, siblings, friends, etc.).

> **Example:** What would happen if you experienced a cyberattack and your smart home was compromised, limiting what you could do in your home? Or if you wired $40,000 to a third party thinking you were sending it to the title company for a real-estate closing when a cybercriminal had been lying dormant on your computer since you connected to the local Wi-Fi at the airport and just made off with the funds?

If everything in your smart home is connected, it is important to have some type of cyber coverage to provide guidance and financial support if your home is ever a target of cybercrime.

> **Examples:** A cybercriminal could hack into your digital locks and change the code or, more seriously, tap into your baby camera or your virtual assistant (i.e., Alexa/Echo that sits on most counters across the U.S.) to listen in to obtain financial or personal information.

For some individuals, there is not enough coverage available on the market to properly protect their true cyber exposure. That is when cyber hygiene is imperative. What is cyber hygiene? Basically, it is the steps and safety precautions one takes to maintain and improve online security.

It's important to discuss how to have good cyber hygiene when you search the web, travel, and navigate a host of everyday situations. Here are a few tips to help get you started on better cyber hygiene:

- A **virtual private network (VPN)** is one of the best ways to protect yourself while online. VPN encryption hides your IP address and protects personal data. Many different providers offer a wide range of VPN services to fit most people's budget and protection needs.

- **Dual authentication** is becoming more common and requires the user to receive a code, photo, or second piece of identifying information after entering their password. This helps to determine whether your computer was hacked or your passwords exposed. Dual authentication provides a second layer of protection to prevent a criminal from accessing your personal information.

  - While the extra step can feel like it slows you down, just think how your life would be interrupted if you experienced a cyberattack. If dual authentication is not automatically included in the online systems you use, talk with the company about how to add this to their login process.

  - When you are sending money, make sure to have a verbal authentication in place as well to ensure there is no misunderstanding when requesting funds via email as that is an easy target for cybercriminals.

- Bluetooth is great. It allows you to listen to your favorite music anywhere you go and talk with people while keeping both hands on the steering wheel. It is important to understand that connecting to Bluetooth in public can leave you vulnerable to a cyber breach. Did you know that criminals can hack into your vehicle's Bluetooth, allowing them access to your devices connected to that specific vehicle? This is why connecting to Bluetooth in a rental car can increase your likelihood of a cyber loss.

- Be careful with whom you share W-Fi password for your home or your hotspot, since that is what gives access to your home network and can allow hackers into your digital universe. If you share your Wi-Fi code with your children or guests, make sure to set up two different internet networks to ensure that you are not doing your banking/investing on the same network to keep your information secure.

There is a lot going on in the cyber world, and sometimes you may find yourself in personal cyber trouble for potential bullying or leaving an exaggerated review about a business. In the litigious world we live in, it is only reasonable to consider what protection is needed should your online activity find you in hot water.

And don't be fooled—not all cyber coverage is created the same, so it is very important that you read the policy form and understand what you are buying ahead of time. Usually there are sub-limits to certain exposure like the extortion limit, but some companies offer full limits. With the right cyber insurance policy, these are some of the coverages you would receive:

- Cyber attack
- Cyber extortion
- Cyber bullying
- Online fraud

Friendly reminder: The internet and emails are *not* always secure. Do not send sensitive information such as your Social Security number, credit card numbers, and banking information via email. This increases your likelihood of a cyber breach. The number of people who blithely email their credit card number or bank routing and account number is jaw-dropping. DO NOT DO THIS!

TRAVEL

Some of our best memories come from traveling. You should be able to enjoy all aspects of your adventures without worry. Whether it is within the U.S. or to different countries, your insurance coverage should provide you with peace of mind and the knowledge that you are prepared should the unexpected happen. Before you take off for your travels, ensure your personal insurance combines coverage and risk mitigation.

Consider these tips when designing a program:

1. Not all liability coverage is worldwide. Some insurance companies only provide coverage in the U.S. and its territories. If you are someone who explores outside the U.S., invest in the right insurance policy that provides worldwide liability coverage so that if something happens and you are held liable, you can rely on your insurance to help guide you and pay the damages.

    Scenario: You are in a hurry to get to your time slot at the Eiffel Tower and rush out of your hotel room and leave the bathroom tap running. You inadvertently flood your hotel room and the unit below yours. Depending on the hotel's policy, you could be held responsible for this damage and required to pay. This accident could easily add up to six figures for damages to the building, property, and lost income while those rooms are being repaired. With the right insurance, you would have personal liability protection.

2. As mentioned in Chapter 5, if collecting valuables while you travel, it is important that your policy offers coverage for newly acquired items. (There are limitations to this coverage, so check specific limits in your policy.)

3. If your personal auto policy has full coverage, liability coverage is usually easily extendable to rental vehicles in the U.S. This is not always the case, however, when renting vehicles outside of the U.S. It

is necessary to have at a minimum worldwide liability on your auto and umbrella policy. Be sure to check with the car rental provider prior to the trip to make sure no exclusions apply.

Renting a vehicle to use off-road or on a racetrack is typically not covered on your personal auto policy.

4. There is no bigger scare than being severely injured away from home or, worse, while out of the country. Travel insurance can help provide excess medical coverage while you travel to make sure you can get the right medical treatment. Confirm that you have travel assistance for replacement travel documents, legal referrals, trip delay/interruption, analysis of your travel risk, and political evacuation. If you're an avid traveler, consider an annual travel policy and make sure it covers both business and pleasure travel if you combine your work and personal travel.

In rare circumstances, the country you're visiting might not honor U.S. insurance. Be sure to verify when renting a vehicle or signing a rental agreement for lodging that the entity accepts U.S. coverage.

When traveling, the last thing you want to experience is loss. These are a few risk mitigation tips to help avoid or limit losses:

1. Don't broadcast your travel plans. Sharing your itinerary can be an invitation for burglars to come into your home or other ill-intending people to take advantage. Kidnapping and ransom are real threats in today's world, with even bigger concerns outside the U.S. Consider adding protection to your homeowners program for some of these possibilities or a travel policy to make sure you have the right resources.

2. Ideally you should be able to enjoy wearing your favorite jewelry while also traveling to your favorite places. However, it is not a good idea to showcase your collection while traveling. Hotel safes are not

as secure as you might think. Flashy items can draw street criminals to you for a quick scare and grab. It is best to limit the valuables you travel with and wear costume jewelry instead.

3. Traveling can increase your likelihood of cyberattacks as well. While you travel, it is extremely important to be prepared with hotspots including VPN and to remember your cyber hygiene. If you are booking lodging, transportation, and activities, make sure they have a secure portal for payments and that you are not emailing payment information.

Some tips that fall outside the realm of personal insurance but are important to keep in mind before you start your next travel adventure include:

1. Save electronic copies of identification, passport, and other necessary travel documents to a secure cloud.

2. Understand if life insurance excludes any of the activities you will be participating in. Examples include scuba diving or skydiving, which can be exclusions within certain forms.

3. If you still have children who look to you to help make decisions (specifically health) and are over the age of 18, make sure you have a medical power of attorney to speak with medical facilities if they are injured and can't make decisions for themselves. Or if you are leaving children at home, make sure the guardian in charge has medical decision documents and that your executor or personal representative knows where your last will and testament or other estate-planning documents are located (heaven forbid something goes seriously wrong and they don't have the documents they need).

FAMILY COMPOSITION: UNDERSTANDING WHO AND HOW YOU ARE INSURED

Families come in all sizes, relationships, and geographic areas and can sometimes be an involved, complicated web. Examples include kids staying on parents' payroll into adulthood, shared assets like homes and businesses, and wealth being passed down from generation to generation. How a family is structured and how their risk overlaps can create a gray area within insurance coverage, resulting in loss exposure.

Typically, insurance is designed to insure a single family residing in the same home. In the last few decades, that is not always the case. Consumers may assume they have coverage in place where they don't based on the simple definition of **covered insured**. The definition for insured is usually one of the first items outlined in the actual policy form (behind the declaration pages), and it dictates to whom and how the policy will respond.

As children grow up, it is important that their insurance grows with them. When they are in college, it is important to consider where their vehicle is garaged, if anyone else will be driving the vehicle, and how the vehicle is titled. If the child is away at school more than 100 miles away without a vehicle, there is a nice discount because they are seen as occasional drivers (see Chapter 3 for additional details on which factors matter).

And as children grow out of the household, they are simultaneously outgrowing their parents' insurance policies. It is imperative that children who no longer reside in the household full-time have their own insurance policy because coverage becomes limited for drivers who are listed but are not residing in your home.

Most people put off making the move off their parents' policy because there is an increase in cost when first going on your own insurance policy. Children going on their own:

- Tend to lose discounts like multicar, multidriver, and multipolicy discounts that they received on their parents' policy.
- They have limited insurance history for the carriers to base their rate on.
- The zip code in which the vehicle will be garaged is a big premium driver, especially if in a different state.

If you leave kids on your policy and they do not live in the household, they have limited coverage for times of uninsured/underinsured coverage, i.e., when they are pedestrians and cyclists along with when renting cars. These limits and enhancements are available to household members but not always to listed drivers. And these are just a few of the many limitations we see when someone is only a listed driver.

What happens when we enter our "golden years"? What should be considered? Typically, four major events occur that require insurance updates:

1. Changes to home occupancy:

   - If the home will be vacant due to the individual moving to a retirement facility, a change in the insurance policy is required.

     - Notify the insurance company as soon as you are aware of the change in occupancy. Depending on the carrier, the policy can remain unchanged until its renewal date. It then will be canceled, and new coverage will need to be found that covers vacant properties (refer to Chapter 1 for coverage information).

     - Obtain a renters policy for the location where the insured will be staying. This will help cover the personal property they have in the unit and, most important, their personal

> liability in case they damage the unit or the facility itself, for example, backed-up toilets, stove fires.
>
> – If property is going to be stored off premises, i.e., in a storage unit, there is typically only 10% of your personal property coverage extended from the renters policy. Based on how much property will be kept at an off-premises location, look to obtain coverage with a carrier that offers 100% of personal property coverage off premises or add a storage location to the renters policy and specific limit for property in that unit.

- Being able to remain in your home for as long as possible is important. And should you bring in support to help you do that, consider the additional risk and potential insurance coverage like workers' compensation, employer's liability, and employment practice liability that may need to be added to your program (refer to the earlier "Employing Persons" section and to Chapter 4 for more information).

2. Selling or gifting an automobile or letting others drive your car

- As you start to age, you may decide to sell or gift your vehicle to a friend or family member. It is important that you update the title immediately and provide a proper bill of sale to help limit and eventually eliminate your liability should the individual cause an accident in the vehicle. How the vehicle is titled matters—you do not want to get dragged in for ownership of a vehicle you thought you no longer owned because paperwork wasn't executed. Once you have confirmation that your name is off the title, you can cancel the auto coverage, but do not do so until you have proof of a new title.

- If you will have someone driving your vehicle on a regular basis to help with day-to-day tasks and driving you around town, you will want to add them to your auto and umbrella policies so there is no gray area if they cause an accident while operating your vehicle.

3. Gifting collections

    As people age, it's common to begin to give away possessions. If you decide to start gifting assets like jewelry, art, and other items, make sure to update your policies accordingly. Advise the individuals to whom you gifted the items to obtain their own insurance. Your insurance will not extend coverage to others once you gift them the item.

4. When a single (unmarried) individual passes and their assets are in the process of being transferred, it's important to understand new limitations that may exist.

    - Auto/Watercraft/Recreational policies: The vehicle, watercraft, or recreational vehicle should not be driven until it is added to a new auto policy. This is because the policy that is in the name of the deceased person becomes void as they can no longer give permission for individuals (not listed on the policy) to drive the vehicle, which some insurance companies use as a way to avoid paying claims.

    - Homeowners: Depending on what happens to the home, if it will be sold, a family member moves into it, or it becomes a rental property, it is important to discuss the update in usage and update the named insured to the correct individual or entity as the policy will only provide coverage (property and liability) for the named insured who has now passed, and the policy could end up providing no coverage for the people who need it.

Then there are the individuals who have no blood relation to us and are part of our life, maybe someone who has naturally moved in or, for instance, a foreign exchange student. Don't assume coverage automatically extends to these individuals.

- If they are going to be living in your home for a long time, talk to your advisor about possible changes to the policy to cover them.
- Consider asking them to purchase renters insurance for personal property and personal liability.
- If the individual will be living in your home and driving your vehicles, they should be added to the auto policy.

Whether it is kids growing up or adults, parents, and grandparents going through life's next transitions, it is important to understand how relationships increase liability. Make sure deeds/titling match the named insured on the insurance policy—there must be financial interest from the named insured in the asset (home or vehicle, etc.) for insurance coverage to apply at the time of a claim. If the insurance policy and title do not match, coverage may not apply.

When it comes to assets being owned by an LLC or trust, some attorneys feel the homeowners policy should be written with that entity as the primary named insured. This is something that may not always be in your best interest.

- LLCs are member-owned entities, and homeowners policies cover individuals. Keywords that do *not* align are **members** *and* **individuals**, which are what cause the ultimate disconnect between policy language and how coverage is considered at time of a loss. If the homeowners policy is written in the name of an LLC, the homeowner (individual or family) will need to have themselves named as an additional insured.

- Personal property is another piece that needs to be considered. Unless you plan to purchase all your clothing, furniture, etc., in the name of the trust/LLC, you will have limited coverage for the property on the homeowners form.

If the homeowners policy does end up being written in the name of an entity, purchase a second policy, which would likely be a renters policy, to cover personal property and liability as the homeowners insurance written in the name of the entity would not provide personal protection.

AIRCRAFTS

Aircrafts range in type, size, and use from personal aircrafts, helicopters, and jets to drones and hot air balloons. What you fly matters and can add additional considerations to your risk program. We will explore this at a high level as most aircrafts fall within the commercial insurance coverage space, but it is important to understand how it may limit personal liability.

Do you own an aircraft? Or is it part of a fleet? Do you occasionally rent a plane? Or are you a pilot? How you participate in the aircraft's usage is another part of the program dynamic.

Also, where you take off from and where you are going matters. Where do you store the plane? If you have a hangar and airstrip on personal property, understand where the commercial aircraft policy ends its liability coverage and where your personal policy would pick up coverage. Also, if you are going to travel internationally, there are different security and safety measures along with documents and liability limits that may need to be met that should be confirmed before takeoff.

If you plan to charter the plane, how you book matters. Typically, planes are booked through a charter broker or independent operator. It is extremely important that, regardless of how you book, you vet the operator and they meet specific standards. Some standards to consider are:

- The rating and the organization they are registered with
- Role separations between safety officer and chief pilot
- Understanding the charter agreement, emergency plan, and flight qualification for the specific flight you will be taking

Most importantly, check that the plane and operator have insurance in place and that you review and understand the coverages.

Last, while you are in flight, don't forget your cyber hygiene. The plane's Wi-Fi may not be secure. You don't know who will be the next guest or be cleaning and refueling the aircraft and whether they are able to execute a cyber breach.

If you decide to go the route of ownership, how you own the aircraft matters. Some people may own the aircraft individually, while others may be part of a flying club, but most fall into the category of partial ownership. How one categorizes it also matters to the IRS. "Co-ownership" and "partnership" are not the same thing for the concepts in this book or to the IRS. **Partnerships** are designed to generate a profit, whereas with **co-ownership**, your intent is to own a plane with another individual.

Like any asset, there are different ways to set up the ownership structure. Typically, we see LLCs, unincorporated associations, and corporations as entity structures for co-ownership. It is extremely important that you engage an attorney who is familiar with aircraft, as there are positives and negatives to each entity structure and tax implications that can come into play.

Before we wrap up this section, I want to address a couple other aircraft and flying exposures:

- **Drones** come with additional regulations and usage liabilities. It is important to understand when the drone outgrows personal liability coverage and would need to be considered on a commercial form. Drones that are FDA regulated or used for business purposes (like inspections or photography) require commercial coverage.

- **Hot air balloons**, even if used for pleasure, are typically excluded on personal insurance and require commercial coverage.

WATERCRAFTS

Being on the water can be one of the most peaceful places in the world, especially as a guest on a boat. However, owning a boat comes with a lot of responsibility, not only in the maintenance of the boat but also in increased liability.

How you use your boat matters. Is it truly a pleasure watercraft from which you sometimes fish, or do you like to make waves and pull loved ones behind you in the tube or on water skis and a wakeboard? Maybe you like to race your boat or charter others for their pleasure.

It's important to consider what happens when things go wrong and to anticipate those scenarios when crafting your personal risk program. Watercraft is another category that can be covered personally or commercially depending on the use and size of the vessel.

The mooring location may necessitate additional risk mitigation requirements. For example, most insurance companies request evacuation plans in highly catastrophic areas to ensure there is a plan to limit damage to watercraft in the event of a storm.

There is also a "layup credit" that can be added if you live in an area that has a boating season versus year-round usage.

If you **charter a boat**, it's important to consider the following:

- Your personal insurance most likely does not provide coverage while charting a yacht. Protection would need to be purchased through a Yacht Charterer's liability policy, which provides protection for damage done to the vessel, fines accrued during the charter, and other liability exposure that may arise. As a charterer or passenger, you hold a lot of decision power, which can become a liability, so it is important not to abuse that and listen to the captain and crew's recommendations.

- Proper visa documentation is imperative for port authorities. Otherwise, fines can be assessed.

- If you are on a bareboat (no captain or crew provided with the vessel), understand the responsibilities that come along with hiring a crew for the voyage.

Note: Don't take this information as the final word for being a prepared charter guest—this is just the tip of the iceberg. Engage a maritime attorney and yacht expert to help navigate the contract and situation that may arise before, during, or after the charter.

If you own a yacht that will be used for charters, it is not a simple business. It requires planning, financial backing, and marketing strategy. Considerations include picking the vessel, its storage location, on which waters it will be sailed, the crew composition, and the management of the charter organization. And, most importantly, when do you plan to use the vessel? Are you okay with working your schedule around the primary boating season?

Talk with an attorney and insurance advisor who specialize in yacht protection before you approach a yacht broker. Understand what you are looking for; otherwise, you might get caught in the moment and find yourself with a liability and money pit.

For the **houseboat owners**: This is a small niche in the market, but if your boat is your primary home, consider a boat policy along with renters insurance to cover property and personal liability off the vessel.

ANIMALS

Animals can be an extension of the family or a way to make a living. In addition to what's been covered in Chapter 2, there is even more to consider if your animals are at the center of your world, including a service animal. When animals are part of your lifestyle, it is important to understand the additional coverage that may need to be considered:

- **Liability:** In case someone is injured by the animal (as discussed in the Homeowners chapter)

- **Mortality:** If you are seeking financial reimbursement should the animal pass away due to a covered loss and must be replaced (i.e., a trained seeing eye dog)

- **Medical insurance:** Coverage for animals can help offset some veterinary costs that arise in daily ownership of animals.

As discussed in previous chapters, if you own animals, a standard insurance program may not work for you. You need to be clear about the details surrounding your animals when obtaining coverage.

Horses/Farm Animals

There is a fine line between what is considered a hobby farm and acceptable on a personal form and what is considered a working farm that requires a farm policy specifically, which is more in line with coverage in commercial insurance. The details around the animals determine which policy works best for your needs, i.e., how many of each specific animal is owned, where they are kept (at home, second residence, or boarded), and usage and value of the animal.

- Breeding and rescuing animals can create issues.

- Exotic animals are a typical exclusion in liability policies, so it is important to discuss the types of animals on premises when building the insurance program.

- Sometimes modifications are made to a home to accommodate animals (for example, built-in fish tanks). This should be considered from a loss perspective and understanding of how insuring water damage may be covered. In general, additions/changes made to a home for animals should be discussed in planning.

It is important to also consider if the animals are a business venture. In that case, they will need coverage from a commercial carrier. Animals that should be covered by a commercial carrier include:

- Animals that are used for competition: Consider the additional items that come along with this venture and may need to be covered.

- Animals that are used for breeding: What are the legal ramifications if something goes wrong?

- Animals that are used as companions for therapy and daily activities:

  - If you have a need for a companion animal, what liability coverage is needed while the animal is on other premises?

  - Be clear on the difference between therapy animals that visit locations and dogs that provide 24/7 support.

COMMUNITY SERVICE

Most of us donate time to a cause without thinking twice. Why would you? You're helping the community. Unfortunately, when you volunteer or offer your time to a nonprofit, there are personal liabilities to which you can expose yourself by participating. And don't assume that the organization you are volunteering with has insurance or that the directors and officers coverage for the nonprofit board you sit on is adequate protection. (If you need a refresher on the D&O exposure, refer to the "Umbrella Verses Excess Liability" section in Chapter 4.)

If you host parties to help raise funds for organizations, campaigns, etc., consider who will be on the premises and what will occur (i.e., activities like bingo to generate money or liquor sales to support a GoFundMe campaign). Consider a special events policy to provide coverage for guests and liquor liability during the function.

If you act as a trustee for your parents or others, understand there are exposure such as being sued for self-dealing, breach of fiduciary duty, and losses for failure to maintain insurance on real personal property and other mismanagement of trust assets. As a trustee, you can be personally liable based on the decision you make.

Chaperoning an event is another activity individuals agree to do without much forethought. Whether chaperoning a field trip, a senior spring break, or helping to keep an eye on kids at a birthday party, if someone is injured or something goes wrong, you could be named in a lawsuit. Even if faced with a frivolous claim, with the right liability coverage, your defense costs will be covered.

At the end of the day, whether you are being a good community member or a friend helping a friend, good intentions can lead to negative outcomes. Depending on your role in the situation, you can find yourself in an unanticipated liability predicament. So, before you raise your hand to volunteer, join another board, or help chaperone a group of kids on spring break, check with your insurance advisors about potential coverage adjustments needed to protect you should things go wrong.

Liability not only increases when you participate in community activities, but everyday pastimes can also leave you responsible for damages. Activities like hunting, recreational sports, and live-action role-playing games, for instance, all have the potential for injuries or damages arguably attributable to your conduct. This is why your personal liability is so important. Whether you own, rent, or couch surf, you should have a minimum of a renters policy with some sort of personal liability coverage to provide defense cost and ability to pay for damages a judge may find you responsible for. Because let's face it, if you've learned anything in this chapter, it's how attorneys keep busy and there is a potential lawsuit in all you do. I kid. But I do hope you feel more confident in understanding and weighing the potential risk of certain activities and how they can affect your personal insurance program.

IN-HOME BUSINESS

The last common lifestyle characteristics we see are those who operate an in-home business. Whether that's an office, art studio, or day care (for pets, the elderly, or children), what takes place between the walls of your home and how you spend your time there matters. Especially if that activity brings in revenue or additional foot traffic by way of customers, no detail is too small for insurance companies. We'll explore the overlap of business and personal life in more depth in the next chapter, but here are some key things to consider if running a business out of your home:

- How much revenue is generated? This can be an eligibility factor in underwriting your home as each insurance company has its own threshold based on the type of business being operated, and if the monies generated exceed that threshold, it can affect eligibility along with coverages available on the homeowners policy. In that situation, it is best to obtain a business insurance policy to cover your operations.

- Does your business increase foot traffic (whether that's employees or customers)? If the answer is yes, then it most likely falls outside the purview of personal insurance.

- Does the operation increase the likelihood of a loss?

  Examples: Type of art material if you are an artist, construction materials that are flammable, pet-sitting where there are new and unknown animals on premises regularly, and day cares that have a range of exposure to consider. If the answer is yes, be clear and pay attention to exclusions that may be added to the homeowners policy (like an animal liability exclusion if the homeowner is running a pet-sitting business). Typically, this gap is easily fixed by purchasing the right commercial insurance coverage.

- Do you keep business property on the premises? If yes, read your homeowners policy carefully, as usually there is limited coverage, maybe $5,000, for business property like desks and items used in an office to operate a business. This would exclude software systems. It is best to purchase a commercial policy to cover business property. The cost to add it is minimal.

- If the business is being run by a child/minor in the household, it is important to understand the liability that comes along with the business and if there are any restrictions with the homeowners policy. Think possible risks with a side job like grass cutting—a home or vehicle could be damaged when a rock ricochets when the mower hits it and breaks an atrium or car window. Another situation: Your child is babysitting, and a child is injured while your teen sitter is texting, and the parents come after your child for negligence. Does your homeowners insurance cover that?

When it comes to life, don't let this chapter deter you from living it to the fullest. Continue to allow your lifestyle to be of your choosing. Just make sure your insurance policy is addressing what makes your life yours. And remember, this chapter highlights just some of the many lifestyle characteristics to consider when building your personal risk program. That is why it is important to work with knowledgeable insurance advisors, so they know when your lifestyle requires additional consideration to avoid gaps in coverage that may expose you to unknown risk and financial loss.

Chapter 7

The Line Between Business and Personal Activities

Business owners tend to work hard and play harder. And why not? Just make sure that you understand whether you are having fun on business time (expensed) or personal time. Because if a loss occurs, how you behave (as employer, employee, or typical citizen) can dictate what insurance responds and what assets can be considered unprotected if insurance limits are exhausted.

The type of business you own can affect personal underwriting as it may increase liability. Thus, it is important that you disclose your business affairs when discussing your personal insurance program.

Just as it is imperative to find someone who specializes in designing your personal insurance program, the same applies to business. A commercial advisor who is a generalist may not be best for your business. In today's digital world, don't be afraid to read reviews to find a commercial advisor who knows your industry. This chapter isn't going to cover commercial insurance per se (that requires a few books of its own) but will address considerations around personal exposures when owning a business and how to limit the mix of personal and business liabilities. I'm not providing legal or accounting advice either but will point out areas to consider and discuss with qualified business insurance professionals.

One of the hardest parts about owning a business is all the decisions and details to consider and address. Most people open a company because they are great at their specific skill but may find themselves overwhelmed as a business owner. Don't let the unknowns of business insurance scare you into a commoditized product that most likely won't serve or protect the full scope of your business. When discussing your business with an insurance professional, disclose everything you do, even if it's something you do on an as-needed basis. While a lot of brokerages use the same major carriers, within certain brokerages and carriers, there are specialized programs they can offer that are specific to certain industries. These types of insurance companies can provide comprehensive coverage and pricing based on their vast knowledge of the industry and insuring similar risk exposures.

Typically, as a business owner, there are a few individuals in your professional life who help guide you such as an attorney, CPA, money manager of some kind (financial advisor, banker, or both), and others. These individuals are usually very good at their jobs but can sometimes silo themselves in their specific industry. And this is where we see insurance become crucial because the right personal and commercial insurance advisor will ask the right questions and ensure that all pieces of your planning align and are protected based on the insurance contract they are selling you.

The phrase "planning align" refers to the insurance advisor's understanding of how other aspects of your life could affect the insurance contract they are selling you based on exclusions or conditions.

- How the business is titled matters. Is it titled in your personal name, as an LLC, or as a trust? Do these entities have mixed usage, owning personal and business assets within the same entity?

- Are there other contracts in play with individuals or businesses that could pull your personal insurance policies into a lawsuit based on structuring of your personal and/or business ventures? If so, this could become an issue when looking to obtain personal coverage.

- Last, are funds all moving through the proper channels rather than being mixed between business and pleasure?

At the end of the day, insurance is just another contract, but unlike most, it is ambiguous, and every piece of a claim matters. That's why understanding how things work up front is important to understanding how and where coverage will respond on the back end. There is no worse feeling than thinking you are paying for coverage only to find out at the time of claim that your in-home business triggered an exclusion on your homeowners and the fire that was caused because you left the machine on overnight left you with no personal coverage.

Other issues we see are **LLCs** and **trusts** that are created but then not fully implemented. An example: Assets are moved to a trust, and the entity (or trust) is not added to the insurance coverage. This omission potentially leaves the entity exposed and not protected by the personal liability coverage in the homeowners or umbrella coverage. This oversight leaves the insured to pay out of pocket for defense costs for that entity as a lot of insurance carriers require the trust or other entity to be listed as a named insured to be covered. Paying for an attorney on your own to defend an entity adds up quickly. In addition, how that trust or LLC is structured could determine if it is eligible to be added to the personal policies. Usually, things get complicated when there are too many members or trustees, and the liability is created based on others' involvement. An additional problem in this context is commingling of different entities and personal assets.

Avoid using the same entities such as an LLC or trust for both business and personal activities and protection. Insurance contracts are not meant to cross between personal and business protection, and the policies include exclusions or limit coverage if used in a manner outside the intent of the contract.

RENTAL PROPERTY

Rental property titling is another area in which it is key to make sure all your ducks are in a row. Holding rentals under your personal name dramatically increases your personal liability. Talk with an attorney about the right entity structure, and make sure to understand how you need to operate to stay in compliance with it. That is the other common issue when individuals don't follow the guidelines and end up exposing personal assets to collection for a company debt through a creditor's attorney "piercing the corporate veil." That means a court does not see the company as separate from the members, owners, or shareholders, who can now be held personally liable for the judgment/debt based on improper execution of that entity's legal formalities.

The right entity in any business endeavor is crucial. Don't take the organization structure lightly, and consult with a professional to get the protection and outcome desired from that entity. And when you choose the entity for your business, understand what is needed to operate and not allow a creditor to pierce the corporate veil you attempted to use.

Example of piercing the corporate veil: A client sets up an LLC for their rental properties but uses their personal credit card (instead of the business one) to pay the annual insurance bill. This could be seen in the court of law as not respecting the separateness of the person and entities and allow the piercing of the corporate veil, thus exposing the client's personal assets. Because personal assets were used to pay the premium for that business and since funds have been mixed to support the business in the past, the personal assets can be looked at to pay debts.

Sometimes an individual wants to write something off as a business expense that mixes business and pleasure. Understand the liability the business is open to by financing that activity and if the risk of that activity opens the business to unnecessary exposure.

HOSTING BUSINESS ACTIVITIES

That leads to the next consideration—hosting business activities. Whether at a personal residence or your personal yacht, hosting, while always generous, opens a multitude of liability concerns including injuries, food poisoning, and liquor liability, to name only a few.

Hosting work entertainment at venues you don't own can help alleviate some of the liability risk (if the establishment has the right insurance in place). Confirm the establishment has general liability and liquor liability (if liquor will be served) at a very minimum. Don't just assume the establishment has the right coverages, as you'd be surprised where some places cut corners. It's a simple ask that can help limit your liability and give you the peace of mind to enjoy your guests' company.

If you choose to host at your home, it's important to take the right measures to protect yourself. Talk with your advisor about the specific event that will be hosted to make sure all the right safeguards are in place. Consider coverage like a **Special Events Policy** with host liquor along with hiring insured bartenders to serve the drinks and caterers for the food.

VEHICLES

Vehicles are another common area where business and personal activities tend to get muddied. Mixing the two without understanding the liability of doing so can bring unwelcome consequences. A common practice is to title vehicles in the business name to use as tax write-offs. However, the name on the title carries a lot of weight in who and what assets can potentially be considered in a lawsuit as collectible assets. As covered in Chapter 3, if a vehicle is truly used for business, title it appropriately. However, if your family members use it most of the time for pleasure, title it personally. This will limit the business possessions from being seen as assets subject to execution after a lawsuit involving a bad car accident where policy limits are exhausted.

Maybe you do not have a personal auto policy and all your vehicles are in a business name on a commercial policy. Typically, there is limited, if any, personal coverage provided in the commercial policy. Consider the following situations, and if they apply to you, consider additional coverage options for personal needs, such as a nonowned auto policy.

- If renting vehicles, make sure there is coverage added to the commercial policy, as this is not always automatically included. If no coverage is provided through the commercial auto, it is important to purchase the liability and physical damage coverages through the rental car company.

- What is covered under uninsured/underinsured motorist coverage could be different on the commercial auto verse personal coverage.

- Do gaps exist with personal excess liability based on no underlying personal auto protection?

- Consider whether family members are driving the car. If yes, consider how that could expose your business.

At the end of the day, it's imperative that your financial team (CPA, attorney, financial advisor, and insurance advisors) for both personal and business meet on an annual basis to make sure all your documents align and that the plans are being executed on all levels.

Note: If you are one of these financial team members, don't forget to find a trusted insurance advisor to support your client's personal and business needs. And don't assume your personal insurance person can handle all your clients' commercial needs. Find a few you trust and on whom you can rely based on the niches you serve. Sometimes personal and commercial insurance can be your safety net in knowing all the planning you are doing with clients is being protected. Don't let a bad insurance decision or oversight undo potential years or decades of planning and business reputation.

PERSONAL INJURY

Last, as a business owner, your words matter. Make sure that one slip of the tongue or keyboard warrior moment doesn't jeopardize what you are building personally but also professionally. Protect yourself with the right insurance coverage for yourself and your business so that if you find yourself in an unfortunate situation, you're not left vulnerable. On the personal lines side, this is typically covered by personal injury.[3] If the comment is made online, cyber coverage will likely come into play.

Quick decisions such as acting in a certain, ill-considered way or even loaning a vehicle in which the driver accidentally kills someone can lead to staggeringly distressing consequences. The simplest decisions can end up tearing the biggest hole in your planning and life. And when you are a business owner, there are important gray areas that cannot be overlooked. Sustaining a personal loss or business loss as a business owner is hard enough, but having a loss on both fronts seems unimaginable. Unfortunately, it happens more than people think.

---

3 In the insurance context, "personal injury" generally refers to claims of defamation, slander, false arrest, malicious prosecution, invasion of privacy, etc.

Take the few hours a year to make sure your ecosystem is aligned and all your hard work, business, and personal financial documents align.

Chapter 8:

Measuring Your Lifestyle Risk and Personal Risk Tolerance

This book has discussed in detail transferring risk to insurance, but what about the pieces of your life you have control over—from the daily choices you make to what you are comfortable "insuring" yourself? This chapter will cover how to better understand your risk tolerance and help design a program to fit you specifically. Most importantly, it will help you apply what you've learned in the prior chapters.

Insurance is a numbers game, and finding the right balance between covering the financially devastating losses and what you are comfortable writing a check for is the key.

LIFESTYLE RISK

It can be hard to take a step back and assess your own life and to know what questions to ask to properly cover yourself. Like most consumers, you may assume "insurance covers it." And as you've learned, that is simply not the case. Insurance is a contract, and the details matter. There are a hundred to a thousand questions that need to be asked about each person's life to ensure your coverage will protect you when you need it and expect it. These 20 yes-or-no questions will help you start to understand how your day-to-day activities affect your personal program.

1. Do you participate in a nonprofit as a director or officer (member)?
2. Do you travel outside the United States for pleasure?
3. Do you have children in your household?
4. Do you have animals in your household?
5. Do you engage in online purchases, online banking, form filing, and other digital engagement?
6. Are any properties that you own deeded in a legal entity (LLC, trust, etc.)?
7. Do you have at-home support with tasks like cleaning, exterior care, cooking, and/or childcare?
8. Will there be any remodeling occurring at any locations that you own?
9. Do you host gatherings at your home(s), such as birthday parties, Friday game night, and/or work holiday parties?
10. Do you operate a business (of any sort) on your property?
11. Do you have a smart home?

12. Do you have regular access to vehicle(s) that you don't own? Consider vehicles such as corporate cars or those of family members you use for an extended period.

13. Are there any recreational vehicles in your household or that you own? Examples include ATVs, golf carts, scooters, and electric bikes.

14. Do you own one or more aircraft?

15. Do you own one or more watercraft?

16. Do you have valuable collections of any type?

17. Have you had any claims in the last 5 years?

18. Do you volunteer in your community?

19. Do you participate in the sharing economy (i.e., renting your home or car, or acting as a driver for people or food)?

20. Are you considered high-profile (recognizable) within your community or beyond? Do you anticipate your status changing to a more "known" status in the coming year?

The questions you answered yes to are the ones that you need to discuss with your agent to better understand what coverage is provided in your current policy or may need to be added to better protect the activities in which you engage.

In addition, the recommendations for some of these lifestyle exposures change by state. **Example:** In some states, a small amount of workers' compensation is provided in the homeowner policy for the occasional employee, whereas in other states, there are exclusions within the liability coverage for when people are working on premise. It is important to understand how your coverage changes based on the state where the employee will work. In addition, every state has different laws about what is considered available for collection by a creditor, so be sure all your planning and documents take those specific laws into consideration.

Note: When your life spreads across states or continents, it is important to work with an insurance professional who can manage your entire insurance program and avoid having three or four insurance agents in different states that are "local." With too many agents involved, major gaps may occur in programs, and consumers end up spending more time "managing" these policies than necessary.

Remember, the above questions are just a starting point. The answer to even one of these questions could change the basis of your program, so please consult with a professional and use these questions as a starting point to the topics you discuss with your advisor.

UMBRELLA LIMIT CONSIDERATIONS

What is the right umbrella limit? That's the million-dollar question in insurance. The truth is there is no right limit, but there is a wrong limit.

The wrong limit is one that clearly does not cover your net worth, as that is the bare minimum that should be considered. **Net worth** is another definition that can be somewhat of a rabbit hole, but for simplicity, it is the portion of assets that exceeds your financial liabilities. **Example:** If you own a home and the value is $850,000 and you owe $350,000, you have $500,000 worth of equity in the home that could be seen as collectable by a creditor if your insurance limits are exhausted.

In some states, future assets and earnings can be a source of assets for payment of damages through the courts. In those states, it is important to make sure your umbrella limit takes that into consideration.

And then there are states where individuals who are injured can sue for unlimited pain and suffering. It is nearly impossible to calculate the right limit in those states.

Your answers to the questions regarding participation as a nonprofit director or officer and employment practice liability (household employees) could limit the carriers you should work with. Only a handful of carriers offer these protections as an endorsement on the umbrella liability policies. Make sure to consider these endorsements and explore insurance carriers that offer coverage if your lifestyle calls for it.

There is a belief that the larger the umbrella policy, the more damages an attorney will pursue. The truth is, if an attorney feels the claimant has a case and if you have assets outside your umbrella limit, they will go after them. The benefits of having the right umbrella limit are:

- Defense cost is part of the coverage (typically). You do not have to pay an attorney to protect you and your assets. The insurance company will continue to defend you until a settlement is made. And in most cases with personal insurance, your defense cost does not go against the limit itself, so the insurance company can spend as much as they need on defense and still write a check for your full umbrella limit if need be. Once your umbrella is exhausted, you are not only on the hook for the additional damages, but also your defense costs going forward. Remember, defense attorneys charge by the hour, which adds up quickly.

- The umbrella limit is the insurance company's money, so they are going to fight to pay the right amount and not just write checks to do so. However, if there is a loss that calls for full limits to be paid, the insurance company may be quick to pay the limits if they are within the reasonable range of the claimants' needs. After the umbrella limits are exhausted is when the issue arises, and a judge can look to your personal assets to make the other party whole.

In addition, consider who you spend time with when choosing an umbrella limit. What would happen if someone in your circle of friends is injured at your home, on one of your watercraft, or riding on your ATV and they could no longer work but still had a family to support? Do you have enough liability currently to pay for the damages incurred, your friend's lost wages, and change in lifestyle?

Can you imagine what would happen if your friend's family sued you because you only had a $3 million umbrella but have a $5 million net worth? You would be in court fighting for your hard-earned money that you need to take care of your family. But your friends also need to support their needs and family that are now changed due to your negligence. Unfortunately, people can find themselves in this situation. That's why it is hard to calculate umbrella limits because maybe you don't have a large net worth, but other aspects within your life like your friend group require you to consider higher limits.

Not to be redundant, but liability insurance is one of the cheapest coverages you can purchase and provides the *most* important protection. It protects against the unknown and unpredictable losses that may occur. You never know who might be injured due to your negligence or what property you or your family might damage. With property damage to your home or vehicle, we know the cost it would take to rebuild or replace them. We calculate the replacement cost up front, and with the right auto carrier, you can buy agreed value, so you know the value of your vehicle at time of a total loss before it occurs. But with liability claims, the possibility of loss types is endless, and sometimes damages are hard to fathom, much less quantify.

So, what is the right limit for you? Work with a financial professional to figure out your net worth currently and what it will be in the future. There are also online systems available to help you quickly calculate your net worth along with the liability needs based on your daily activities.

FLIPPED RISK TOLERANCE TRAP

Flipped Risk Tolerance (FRT) is very common in insurance but rarely talked about in the right way. Typically, FRT is seen in two places within a personal insurance program: the homeowners and umbrella policies.

Let's define and explain **Flipped Risk Tolerance** so you understand what it is.

Note: Don't confuse your risk tolerance with your risk appetite, which is daily activities or assets for which you assume the risk and are comfortable insuring 100%.

Risk tolerance is the amount of loss (the deductible) an individual is willing to handle while making an investment decision (premium dollars) to shift the unwanted risk (rebuild cost of home, car repairs, large liability loss, etc.) to the insurance company.

FRT is often a misconception on the consumer's part in which they think they have successfully shifted the unwanted financial risk to the insurance company when in reality they've only transferred a portion of the risk to the insurance company. How does this occur?

Here are some factors that lead to the FRT trap:

- The insured is unaware they've fallen victim to this misconception and usually find out at claim time or when they review their coverages with a true insurance professional.

- The buying decision was heavily weighted by premium dollars.

- The insured assumes "it's never going to happen," so they choose "middle of the road" coverage, figuring that if the worst comes to pass, they have some coverage, but they don't want to pay the premium to insure the full value. This is when deductibles can help realign a consumer and take them out of FRT. This is because you can buy the right catastrophic-type coverage but maintain reasonable pricing by increasing the deductible.

- The insured misunderstands the policy language and assumes the declaration means one thing when policy language actually reads differently. We see this a lot with extended replacement cost. Consumers think they can underinsure the home and use the extended coverage to get to the true rebuild cost. However, conditions in the policy language limit this possibility by putting in the coinsurance clause (discussed in more detail in Chapter 2), which sets the condition that the home must be insured, usually between 80% to 100%, to the company's rebuild value for extended rebuild cost coverage to apply. If the dwelling limit on the declarations falls below the set percentage, a penalty is incurred, and some of the "extra" coverages on the policy no longer apply.

An example of FRT in homeowners insurance: Consumers want to forego insuring the home for full rebuild cost, aka replacement cost. Instead, they choose to self-insure the larger, "never-going-to-happen" claims and carry low deductibles with limits that do not protect their assets fully. The reasoning is that when a claim occurs, they don't want to have to write a big check… but remember, you write the premium check every year, and few people experience a claim each year. Instead, the better course of action is to carry a higher deductible, write the higher check if a loss occurs, but annually pay the right premium to cover the larger loss so you don't have to write two checks: the deductible check AND the check to rebuild your home because insurance is not covering the full cost.

Example: Let's say you currently insure your home for $900,000, which is what you purchased the home for (market value), with a $2,500 deductible. However, the home should be insured for $1.2 million, which is the true cost to rebuild the home.

- With FRT, one tends to think that they'd prefer to keep the deductible and premium lower and assume they will never experience a total loss. Along with this, there is a false sense of "comfort" in covering the dwelling for the market value of $900,000 due to the misunderstanding in the different criteria used to calculate the rebuild cost versus the market value, leaving them exposed. Unfortunately, a fire occurs, causing a total loss. The cost to rebuild is $1.2 million, and the insurance company is only going to give you $900,000 (if that). How are you going to come up with the $300,000 deficit to rebuild?

- This is where deductibles become important—especially if you feel you will never use insurance and only want it for larger losses.

- Maybe you are thinking, "It is never going to happen, and if it does, I can write a check for $50,000, $100,000, etc." If that is the case, that should be your deductible, as homeowners claims do not happen often, but if there is a total loss and your home cost $1.5 million to rebuild and you only insure for $850,000 because that is what you bought it for, you are technically self-insuring $650,000. Wouldn't it be better to have insurance up to $1.5 million and carry a $50,000 deductible? That way, you know your max out of pocket, and should the worst-case scenario occur, you can rely on your insurance to cover that larger financial portion.

Don't let a high deductible scare you, especially if you have some savings that you can rely on should the worst happen. Wouldn't you prefer to write a check for $10,000 or $25,000 versus $300,000? Could you even cover the $300,000 deficit that exists at the time of a rebuild?

The second place we see FRT is when the insured does not purchase enough liability coverage and is too focused on spending premium dollars on property coverages that they could potentially be self-insuring.

Here are some claims examples to help you start thinking through how you would handle these situations and what type of tolerance you have. This will also help with the next part of this chapter, which focuses on what deductible is right for you.

How would you handle claims for certain situations? The knee-jerk reaction is to file the claim "because that is what insurance is for." When you use your insurance, you are penalized not only financially but in what options you have in the marketplace based on claims history. The first claim isn't usually an issue, but when there are two or three claims within 5 years, issues arise. We want to save insurance for those must-have situations, not nice-to-have ones.

The best practice is to only use insurance when you specifically need to do so. Here are some scenarios to better understand your risk tolerances and the decision whether to use insurance:

- Your refrigerator leaks, causing $5,000 worth of damage to your kitchen floors.

  Consider this: Remember, water damage is a big red flag in insurance and can trigger additional underwriting in the future along with risk mitigation requirements such as automatic shutoff valves to avoid future water losses.

- An electrical fire starts in your home while you're away for the weekend, causing $600,000 in damages.

- While pulling out of your driveway, you back into your neighbor's car, causing $8,000 in damages.

- A tree falls on your fence, causing $10,000 in damages.

- A kid cutting the neighbor's grass hits a stone that ricochets and breaks your atrium window, causing $3,000 in damages.

- Hail damages your roof to the tune of $35,000. Your roof, however, is 10 years old and you have special language in your policy specific to limited roof coverage. You have actual cash value coverage for your roof, which means the roof is not covered for replacement cost and that depreciation will be taken into account when determining what the insurance is responsible for.

For the sake of this example, let's say your roof has a 20-year life expectancy and is halfway through it; based on it being 10 years old, the insurance company is only going to give you half the cost, which is $17,000 of the $35,000 for the roof, minus your deductible, based on the actual cash value language within the policy.

- Your dog bites your friend's leg and they need medical care, costing $6,000.

  Consider this: If you file this claim, you may have an issue getting liability for animals in the future. The carrier could cancel you or require you to get rid of the dog if you'd want to stay insured.

- You are shooting fireworks off for the Fourth of July when embers from a firecracker land on your neighbor's house, causing a fire and damaging their home and vehicles in the garage, costing $260,000.

- One night after a nice evening out, you place your stud earrings on the sink and forget to put them in your jewelry box. The next morning, you wake up to your toddler playing in the sink and no earrings to be found. The cost to replace them is $9,000.

  Consider this: If there is a frequency of similar loss for valuables, it can be hard to get coverage for that loss type. Too many mysterious disappearance claims could cause insurance carriers not to offer this as a covered loss going forward.

- You have a few friends and their families on your property for the weekend and a child drowns while swimming. The child was a senior in high school and going through recruitment for college sports. You are sued for $5 million.

As you see, life happens, and making sure you are only filing claims when necessary will allow you to use your insurance when you really need to. In some of the examples above, it would be nice to use insurance, especially if you have never used it. But consider if you have an unfortunate year, and maybe a tree falls on your fence and also another unforeseeable event occurs. This just took you from a very insurable household to potentially having limited to no options. You will be left overpaying for inadequate coverage for a minimum of 3 to 5 years while your claims history cleans up.

USING DEDUCTIBLES TO PERSONALIZE YOUR INSURANCE PROGRAM

As discussed, the deductible is one piece of the policy that you can customize your cost based on your risk tolerance. A few other considerations when picking a deductible:

- When a consumer files a claim, there is a cost-benefit analysis. Catastrophic size claims are easy—you should make the claim as that is what it is there for. Smaller claims are more difficult. The insurance companies can surcharge the claim payout over 3 to 5 years, so while the lower deductible makes you think that filing a claim is a good financial decision, it could actually end up costing you more based on the surcharges applied.

- Based on your savings and rainy-day fund, align your deductible with the dollar amount you would feel comfortable writing a check for.

  - Remember, insurance is just another bank, so when you file a claim, you pay a surcharge or "interest on that money" for 3 to 5 years, and those surcharges range. If you can afford to cover a loss out of pocket, it can make sense to avoid using insurance, even if it means using some of your home equity line of credit (HELOC) that you will slowly pay back over time. Those monthly payments could be less than the increase you see on your insurance.

– If you file too many claims, then you are at risk for nonrenewal and limited options in the market. Higher deductibles help you from filing too many claims that are not financially necessary.

• Hopefully you will never have a claim and the need to pay your deductible. Pick a dollar amount you are comfortable with now and, as your savings grow, adjust your deductible accordingly.

Overall, insurance is one of the only things you buy that is a contract that you agree to up front, but then the performance of the contract is sometimes based on hundreds of factors that the consumer does not consider. Exclusions could exist based on lifestyle choices, and then you'll find yourself paying for a piece of paper (bad insurance policy) that doesn't do anything for you. As you put this book's recommendations into practice, I hope you'll avoid those pitfalls.

Chapter 9:

What You Don't Know Could Hurt You

Understanding the nuts and bolts of personal insurance is a first step. And then knowing how to apply what you learned to make immediate changes to better protect everything that makes up your specific lifestyle is the critical next step.

This chapter will help you apply what you've learned and provide insight into common questions to empower you to make efficient and effective decisions for your personal insurance program.

MOST COMMON QUESTIONS

How Do I Pay Less for Insurance? Am I Really "Saving" Money?

You can't turn on your TV without seeing an ad for cheaper insurance. But what's the cost to you? While paying less is tempting, there is typically a reason why a company can offer lower rates over another. Hopefully you fit their target market and your pricing reflects that you're in the company's sweet spot. However, often the "savings" advertised on TV is because the company limits coverage, leaving you feeling that you're being nickel-and-dimed when you make a claim.

Consumers have been misled to believe that insurance is simple and should be an "easy" to-do item to check off the list. And that is the furthest thing from the truth. Insurance is an investment against catastrophic loss. Insurance is complex. It's a contract that can't be read out of context because every part of a claim matters. This is because where coverage is a given when the policy is written, it can be excluded later based on the origin of the damage. Additionally, coverage will only be provided if certain conditions have been met. And a lot of times, claims arise out of lifestyle choices that are typically missed in personal insurance design, leaving one exposed.

Note: Don't fall prey to the assumption that coverage is "apples to apples" when shopping your coverage. What this means is the dollar amounts align, not the policy language (most of the time). That is how and why companies can charge different rates for similar dollar amounts in coverage. The dollar amounts of coverage offered are only a portion of what should be compared. You need to consider the language of the policies. That's why working with an insurance professional can be helpful. It saves you from reading and interpreting insurance policy contracts.

Sometimes consumers outgrow highly advertised carriers based on their lifestyle characteristics. And options to obtain the appropriate coverage are limited based on lifestyle needs. Maybe you are well known (either in your community or beyond). Or your home rebuild cost and/or excess liability needs are north of $5 million. Only a handful of carriers in the market offer these types of limits and can handle a claim properly.

- The key word is *properly*. For example, most of the higher-value homes have craftsmanship and unique building design. Being able to hire the right contractors and designers to restore the house with the original material is the difference between "middle market" insurance companies and the high-net-worth companies. The main difference between companies can be found in the policy language, specifically on how the insurance contracts will repair or rebuild the home. A vast majority of companies offer "*similar* kind and quality coverage"; however, a handful of markets offer "*same* kind and quality." That simple difference in wording can change how you rebuild your home.

- If you live in a historical district or area with strict HOA require-ments, it is extremely important to understand the rebuild/repair requirements for that area to ensure the home policy you purchase will respond to meet your desired requirements. For example, your policy stipulates "similar quality" for your home repair. Based on that language, the insurance company will only offer brick veneer for material rather than the real brick the historical district requires. This language would likely force you to spend additional money outside of your deductible to cover the difference between veneer and brick to comply with the historical requirements.

While no one wants to pay more to an insurance company, it is important not to make quick decisions and cut corners when shopping. When deciding which insurance company to "invest" your money in, take your time and don't base your decision only on the cost of the premium. Because at the end of the day, insurance is an investment. You pay premiums to transfer risk and rely on the insurance company to make you whole again should you experience a loss. Like most things in life, quality insurance comes at a higher premium. Look for an insurance company whose contract aligns with what you are looking to cover and where your expectations will be met should a claim arise.

If you're still weighting your decision heavily on the cost of the premium, there are other factors to consider before jumping to a new insurance company. The two major considerations are:

1. The business process for the company you are moving to. This matters because every insurance company handles new business differently. Here are a few of many factors that may vary:

    - Property inspections are becoming common practice for insurance companies to complete upon issuing new coverage. Typically, the inspections are exterior, but depending on the size of your home, there could be interior inspections required as well. Usually, inspections are not an issue. They're just a way for insurance companies to confirm the risk they are covering and to gather additional documentation should there be a loss to help with the claims process. However, inspections sometimes uncover problems for the homeowner to address. Those action items can be as straightforward as cutting a few branches away from the home, or the roof may be in "unsatisfactory" condition for the insurance company and require that a new roof be installed within a certain time frame. Or an inspection could trigger an immediate notice of cancellation because you have a dog on the premises that is a breed on a list that now makes your home ineligible with the carrier.

    - The insurance company has the ability to immediately cancel due to underwriting information discovered after issuance.

        - Some carriers make a courtesy call for lines of business such as auto and umbrella to make sure the information on the initial application submitted is correct. During that call, you may mention something that was not disclosed on the application, such as an additional household member with a bad driving record. Just like the homeowners inspection, the company can cancel the new policy based on the information.

– The time frame for which a company can cancel coverage and the length of notice they are required to give the consumer varies from state to state. That is why it is important to discuss all your specifics before changing companies.

• You will have to sign an application for the new policy or policies you are buying. While this may seem like a no-brainer, that is not always the case, and the application will be referenced at time of claim to confirm facts that were provided at the start of the policy.

– Do not omit information when shopping, especially when getting quotes online. Be sure to disclose all you have going on in your life, especially if you've been told that said "thing" complicates securing coverage. For example, if you learn that knob/tube wiring is hard to get covered, do not "forget" to disclose that as you shop. Many applications will ask whether there is knob and tube wiring and to confirm other materials of major systems in the home, including plumbing, electric, HVAC, and roofs, when you sign the application, and by not disclosing, you could void the policy.

– When working with an agent directly, it's *very* important to review the insurance application you are signing. Sometimes agents assume the underwriter's answer to certain questions is a "no," or maybe the last time you talked, it was "no," but there have been changes that if not corrected could allow the insurance company to deny a claim.

There are also insurance agents who "forget" to ask certain questions (such as dog breed or type of wiring in your home) as they know it could jeopardize the sale. Their perspective is "other agents don't ask, so why should I ask and lose the sale?" Yes, that is a selfish way to think, but there are agents out there like that.

2. There are specific enhancements and coverages only available with certain insurance companies. It is important to understand what you may lose and not be able to get back if you decide to return to that insurance company later. (An example is the situation described above where an insurance inspection leads to immediate cancellation of the policy. You may want to get your "old" policy back, however, which is not always an option as offerings from insurance companies change.)

- **Deductible savings account:** Some carriers offer the option whereby every 6 months you go without a claim, you earn a credit toward your deductible, and the credit is applied at time of a claim. (Example: If you are with an insurance company for 3 years and have this enhancement and avoid accidents for the 3 years, you would have a $300 credit toward your auto deductible at time of a claim in year 4 of doing business with that company.) If you move to a new insurance company, that benefit is lost, and your deductible goes back to the chosen limit.

- **Grandfathered coverage:** It is not uncommon for insurance carriers to change their policy form. And when they do, they can remove or limit coverage on the new form. The policies written on the old form are typically grandfathered to keep the better coverage. However, if you leave and then want to return to that carrier, you would be forced to use the updated form and could lose some enhancements that were part of the old policy form.

An example of a grandfathered enhancement is guaranteed renewal, which we rarely see in the market now but was part of older contracts and can be very important should you have an unfortunate series of events with multiple losses. This feature requires the insurance carrier to offer renewal terms and eliminates the option to nonrenew your policy and potentially be left uninsured due to claims history.

- **Longevity credits** are important and can be useful if there is an unfortunate situation where a few claims happen to occur back-to-back. Remaining with the same carrier for a longer time may likely help you retain your insurance program with them, even if you experience a series of unfortunate events. If you jump from carrier to carrier, you could quickly find yourself being nonrenewed if you have an unfortunate year with multiple claims.

The best way to not overpay for the coverage you need is to carry a deductible that fits your risk tolerance. By taking on more risk in a high deductible, the insurance company offers better pricing. If you've been with an insurance company for a while and have not reviewed your deductible, that should be part of your "shopping" process to obtain deductible options for the current program.

When choosing the deductible right for you, consider:

- What dollar amount you are "comfortable" or "able" to pay yourself.

- You pay the premium every year but hope to never have to pay a deductible. If you have the means to comfortably pay $10,000 should a claim occur, that is where you set your deductible.

    - There are situations where you can choose or may be required to carry deductibles of 6 or 7 figures, but depending on the risk, that is still worth the trade-off including the peace of mind to have the right insurance company to help you

> rebuild your life should a financially devastating loss occur to your home, vehicle, or other asset you are insuring.
>
> – Sometimes companies offer lower deductibles, which is appealing to the consumer, but the company is not able to offer the right limits for the property damage or liability. The lower deductible/out-of-pocket cost can be tempting but will leave you significantly exposed. Should a claim occur, you will potentially pay a lot more out of pocket at the time of loss than the additional cost in premium for the right coverage with a higher deductible.

- Insurance companies make most of their profit in the stock market from premium dollars. If you are financially savvy or work with a financial team, consider taking the savings by going to a more appropriate deductible or program design and invest the savings in an IRA, high-yield savings, or the market, so not only do you make up the difference in your deductible, but also potentially gain profit from the money since it will be able to sit and grow. Of course, you can also lose money in the market!

Do not automatically accept the deductible. It is important to slow down to consider your comfort level for risk. At what level do you feel comfortable paying for the damages? When do you want to start relying on the insurance company to pay? That leads to the next question: How and when do you use your insurance, and if filing a claim, is it always "worth it"?

"That's What Insurance Is for!" Should You Really File a Claim?

The natural thought is to file a claim because, "This is why I have insurance, right?" While that isn't wrong, it is not that straightforward. Filing a claim isn't as simple as you might think. There are certain situations when moving forward with a claim is a no-brainer. For instance, a fire damages half your home, you come home from vacation to a burst pipe, or you incur a larger liability claim due to someone getting injured at your home. However, every claim is unique, and the details matter because the policy you purchased has conditions and exclusions that easily take away coverage that may be "given" in the covered losses section. A lawyer once told me that, "What the big print giveth, the little print taketh away."

If the loss situation allows, call your insurance agent and work with them to determine the next best steps before rushing to call the 800 claims number and filing a claim with the insurance company. Your agent can help navigate the "pros and cons" of filing a claim, prepare you for the claim process should you decide on that option, and possibly provide third-party service providers to help repair the damage.

When weighing the pros and cons of filing a claim, here are a few things to consider. These points should not be thought of as determinative on their own, but things to simultaneously weigh when faced with damage.

1. Will addressing the damage cost more than my deductible? And not just over but a *decent* amount over. This matters because:

   - You want to make sure that in the long run, the money received from the insurance company does not end up costing you more than what you received on the claim payment. What does this mean? Remember, when you file a claim, most of the time there is a surcharge for 3 to 5 years. Sometimes the surcharge dollar amount over those 3 to 5 years ends up being close to or more than the insurance company actually paid out to you in damages for said claim.

   - The insurance is like a bank, and when you file a claim, you are "borrowing" money at a very high interest rate known as a "surcharge." These surcharges vary based on claim type, the number of claims filed, and other factors. If you can "borrow" money from elsewhere (yourself, savings, etc.), do so as it's cheaper and won't negatively impact your insurance claims history.

2. Is the cause of loss and the damage that occurred clearly covered in the policy?

   - This is when having a relationship with an insurance professional is important as they can help determine this before you contact the insurance company and "officially" document the loss on your record. The policy form you purchased will determine what is and what is not covered.

   - The circumstances surrounding the loss occurred are important not only to determine if the policy will respond but also because the initial damage may not be the only issue. There could be a bigger problem that could complicate future underwriting and renewal issues.

     Example: We see this with plumbing. Maybe one pipe leaks, and the investigation of that leak reveals that all plumbing is bad and needs to be replaced. Is it worth filing a $5,000 claim to replace the plumbing and/or lose coverage? Sometimes understanding how the loss occurred can better prepare you for the next steps and outcome once the insurance company gets involved.

3. Frequency of claims is becoming an issue in today's market. Frequency here refers to how many times you've called the 800 claims number and "filed" a claim, whether the insurance company paid out or if the claim is considered chargeable or not. If you "tried" to use insurance, it is reported to the Comprehensive Loss Underwriting Exchange (CLUE) and used for underwriting and rating purposes. This matters to you because:

   - If you decide to shop for better new insurance or maybe need to purchase more, there are underwriting guidelines around how much "activity" can be on a piece of new business. If there are too many inquiries on the reports, an insurance company won't offer terms.

- Even something seemingly as basic as using your roadside assistance too frequently can hinder you from moving companies or cause your policies to be reevaluated for eligibility by underwriting when your policy comes up for renewal. Overusing this benefit could lead to losing that specific coverage or being nonrenewed. Per the previous point, if you are nonrenewed, you could have a hard time finding new coverage.

- Underwriters look at accounts based on the household, so if a few household members have blemishes on their driving record, this can also cause issues for the other drivers in the household.

  Did you know? In some states, an attorney can help get rid of speeding tickets or have them moved to nonmoving violations. This can save you a lot in insurance premiums and help keep you insurable.

4. Could filing this claim affect the rest of my program?

- When underwriters are reviewing accounts, they typically look at two reports: the CLUE for home property damage and all auto claims. They also run a Motor Vehicle Records (MVR) to see what types of violations are on your auto records. These reports affect *all* lines of business. So, consider situations such as:

  - Maybe you have a lead foot, and you have a few smudges on your record. When you buy your dream car, boat, or ATV, you can't qualify for insurance based on your "bad" driving record. Now you can't leave with your dream car because you legally need insurance to drive.

  - Not being able to get insurance can also limit your ability to get a loan as loans require certain types of coverage to "qualify" for that loan.

- Excess/umbrella liability follows the underlying liability limits, and based on claims history, you may be limited on how much liability you can purchase on auto, homeowners, "toys," etc. If the limits on these policies are too low, you will not qualify for excess/umbrella coverage. This will expose you to larger liability losses and those financial claims you can't cover.

  - You can also limit the amount of excess coverage you can purchase based on the claims history.

  - If you are found at fault for a loss that exceeds your liability limits, an injured party could sue you for additional damages, and if a judge agrees, you will have to figure out how to pay for these additional costs. Solutions might include asset or wage garnishment.

Like most things in life, you get what you pay for, and insurance is no different. The cheaper coverage you were searching for may not be as "cheap" as you thought, and even if the coverage is provided sometimes, you find yourself doing more leg work to "prove" the damage is covered.

As discussed, when shopping for a carrier, understanding the financial stability, claims process, and philosophy of each carrier is important (but can be hard to do on your own). While they usually come from the same base ISO form, every carrier has different policy forms and can enhance or limit coverage within those forms. That's to say that different carriers have broader policy language in favor of the consumer, whereas others have very strict and limited language that leaves the consumer fighting for what they thought they had. When shopping based primarily on price, consider the trade-off for that lower premium. With some insurance carriers, filing a claim can be complicated and sometimes drag on for years. Buying the right coverage from a good carrier can be the difference between quickly moving on with life and having to spend countless hours being nickel-and-dimed.

Consider this:

- What do you make an hour? Use that number and multiply the time you will spend (or maybe have spent) fighting for what you thought you had coverage for. Would spending more each year on the right personal insurance be a good financial investment based on the income you'd lose in time spent fighting for coverage you could have had if you'd invested in the right insurance up front?

- Do you have the time in your schedule to allocate 5 to 20 hours or more to manage a claim, read (and interpret) policy language, and make calls to the adjuster?

  - The right advisor can help manage the claims process and take on the hours sometimes required to go back and forth with adjusters, ensure the claim moves forward, and that you are receiving the full benefit of your policies.

  - Some insurance agent offices have internal claims teams to help navigate larger claims and support the insurance advisor and the client during the claims process. If you want your premium dollars to "work" for you and get the best value for your insurance premium, look for a firm that offers this extra service. Having a claims expert who sets the right expectations for you, knows the nuances of the policy language, and holds the insurance company accountable so you truly have a team on your side is invaluable at the time of a claim.

  - Adjusters are people too, and so working with agents can help keep the process smooth and hold the company accountable. They may interpret language differently. You can either pay a premium to the mass market or work with an agent and have your premiums go toward guidance when you need it at times of claims and life changes.

– When repairing your home, you want to know that who you hire can do a good job. Because the insurance company will *not* pay to have the work redone if you choose a bad contractor, some insurance carriers have preferred partnerships with contractors to help with repairs and even guarantee their work.

Everyone has a different threshold for when filing a claim makes sense. When thinking about your personal life, it's important to remember that insurance is for financially devastating losses. While it may be painful to pay a $10,000 claim out of pocket, in the long run, it could be what is best for you.

Insider's note: It seems that once an insured files one claim, another follows, and while having one small claim isn't the end of the world, two claims regardless of size can cause underwriting issues as discussed. While you may have been claims-free for 20 years, it's still important to be judicious about when to file a claim. If you take a "why not use it" stance, just know that if a large claim comes, that mentality could leave you in a tough spot.

Usually when claims go wrong, it's when the consumer rushed the buying process and assumptions were made on both sides. The insurance agent assumes answers to certain underwriting criteria and coverage the insured wants or does not want. The client assumes the policy may be broader than it actually is or that all insurance is created equal.

This is why you and your neighbors could have the same loss at the same time and have totally different experiences at the time of a claim. Examples include a hailstorm, hurricane, or wildfire. Your neighbor may get a brand-new roof, and you're only offered pennies on the dollar based on your policy being actual cash value for roof damage and the neighbor's coverage is for replacement cost. Not all insurance policies are created equal, and it's important that you find coverage that best aligns with your needs and expectations.

OVERALL TAKEAWAYS

1. If you invest in nice things in life, invest in good insurance.

2. Claims history is a big driver in cost and insurability. If you want to pay the right price with the right company, you need to be considerate of the claims you file and how many you file.

3. Only file claims when financially necessary because your claims record is like your credit report. Once there is a smudge on there, it will affect you for years—anywhere from 3 to 10 years. Typically, we see the 10-year look back in auto insurance for major violations like DWI and DUI or speeding over 20 miles per hour.

Think of insurability like credit. The better credit you have, the lower your interest rates, and with insurance, the lower premiums. You can qualify for things because of credit worthiness. Your insurance claims history works the same way—the fewer marks on your record, the more options you will have. And the better you will perform in the insurance algorithms.

As you've learned, insurance is not as "simple" as commercials make it look. And there is a lot of thought and consideration that should go into building and maintaining your insurance program. While there are the everyday underwriting red flags, the number keeps increasing, and what is a "standard" risk one day could be deemed a "red flag" the next. That is why insurance cannot be an afterthought and must be part of the financial planning process. Otherwise, you could find yourself in an unfortunate situation.

ALL INSURANCE AGENTS ARE NOT THE SAME

Just like policies are not all the same, agents differ as well. The only thing they have in common is they all passed a test to "sell" insurance. And who wants to be sold anything? If you are going to pay for it, don't you want to get the most for your money?

One way to get more for your money is to work with an actual human who understands insurance. While the self-service model is nice and convenient up front, as discussed, the unknowns of the lean policy language could cause a financial headache. If you live a simple life, with limited assets to insure, then the trade-off for self-service may be worth it. However, if your life is somewhat complex, then choosing a broker or captive insurance agent is a great way to get the best value. With a broker or agent, you will get to talk to a person and ask questions about your life to get the best coverage for you. This does not cost you more because insurance companies pay brokers for being representatives of their products through commissions, which is part of the premium you are paying. Typically, direct writers build in marketing dollars to premiums versus commission as they need to spend billions of dollars to drive you to their websites and build trust with you through advertising channels.

You might encounter a good company but bad representatives or a good representative with a bad company. Some people see insurance as a job, while others view it as a career vocation. I want to help you make sure that regardless of the company you choose, you feel comfortable with your decision. To better understand where to buy insurance, it is important to know who you are buying it from. Insurance agents must be licensed to sell insurance for all Property and Casualty; however, the process to get licensed is quick and easy. As a consumer, it's important to know about this low bar to enter the industry. It allows people to go into the business who only want to sell a policy and make a quick buck. They probably don't understand or care about the consumer's risk exposure and are comfortable selling a policy that does not meet all of the clients' needs or expectations.

It is extremely important to work with a professional who understands the insurance contract they are selling you and makes sure your lifestyle does not void or limit coverage within their policies without your knowledge. Both the direct writers and broker insurance carriers support education and have ample opportunities for their agents to engage if they choose. The ones that choose to engage tend to have extra letters behind their name or certificates listed on their website or email signature.

Regardless of the channel you choose, avoid working with "order-taker" agents who exist in all channels of the insurance-buying process. Order-taker agents are those who allow you to dictate the coverage limits. While this may seem ideal, the truth is, you are exposing yourself by doing business this way. Sometimes there are conditions within the policy contracts that need to be met that go against your "ask." An order taker is going to do what you want and then, if something happens, point the finger at you and say, "Well, that's what you asked for" … which is correct. But in reality, you would have preferred to know that your "order" may leave you more exposed than protected. And that is the advice a true insurance professional would give. They are prepared to have the hard conversations to ensure the consumer has the right information up front to make educated decisions concerning their insurance needs (and not point fingers at the time of a claim).

There are many ways to purchase insurance, and the options are only growing. That's great for the consumer because there needs to be diversity of carriers in the marketplace that allow clients to have their needs met at a level at which they are comfortable. The following four are common ways but not the only ways to meet your insurance needs:

1. **Direct Insurance:** The consumer works directly with the insurance company to purchase coverage, usually online or through an 800 number. This may appeal to the "do it yourself" person who prefers to navigate the insurance-buying process on their own. The process is quick and easy—you just go to a website where you select and purchase the coverage all without ever speaking to a live person. There are helpful tips on each coverage to help you make a more informed decision. Usually chat options are available to answer your questions. The main reason people choose this option is because it is the "easiest and cheapest" way to purchase coverage, so why not?

Especially when you see the brands advertised day in and day out and have learned to "trust" them. While the savings are enticing, there are some trade-offs to consider in getting that up-front savings.

Pros:
- These are easy to use with little to no pressure to "buy" anything at the end of the quote.

- You have full control over the quote process with how much coverage you want.

- It is cost-friendly.

Cons:
- There is no personal relationship and little accountability since you speak to a new person each time you call, chat, or email.

- There is little to no guidance around what you may specifically need. You don't know what you don't know, so you could be missing coverage(s) you need.

- When you need to use your insurance, there is no worse feeling than feeling alone, confused, or sometimes frustrated because of what is going on with the claim. With the "self-service" model, you may be spending more time researching and "fighting" a claim based on the misunderstanding of coverages that were or were not purchased based on assumptions.

2. **Captive Companies:** These are companies like State Farm, Farmers, and USAA where the insurance agents represent one company and their products (some do have the ability to work with wholesalers). These companies are common and usually have local agents in the area that manage offices that handle the day-to-day insurance sales and servicing. With captive companies, there is a uniform feel that allows the agents within the office to focus on customer needs while

the home office focuses on business strategies and branding. This is beneficial for the clients as there are standardized products and services they can expect from each company.

Pros:

- The agents are usually community members, and by working with this type of company, you can do business with *people* you know, like, and trust.

- There is the option to self-service and work with a representative when you need.

- Most are established brands with a history that includes current and prior client reviews.

Cons:

- If you find yourself moving states and want to stay with the same carrier, you may have to get a new agent because these companies usually have their local agents segmented by territories and do not allow agents to sell outside their territories.

- Uniform "feel and culture" can be a false sense of security as the offices may not always follow the corporate structure.

- Not all companies are nationwide, so if your life spans across a few states, you may have to work with different insurance companies.

3. **Independent Agents, aka Brokers:** These types of insurance professionals work with multiple insurance companies and can work on the clients' behalf to help select which company is best suited for their needs. Typically, agencies have anywhere from five to 15-plus company appointments, so it is important to understand what relationships they have with the insurance companies. Typical companies that brokers represent are Chubb, PURE, AIG, Cincinnati, Acuity, Hanover, and so on. Often, consumers are not familiar

with these brands as these companies don't spend billions on advertising. Instead, they use the premium dollars to pay commissions to brokers for appropriately placing the right business with them.

Pros:

- The agent works for you, the consumer, not any specific insurance company. They can help shop the markets, provide guidance on claims, and offer out-of-the box solutions as life calls for them. When the broker places business with a company, they are compensated via commissions from the company directly.

  This can be seen as a negative, but most brokers place business based on what is in the best interest of the client, not how much commission they are getting from said insurance company.

- While the up-front time spent providing information to a broker may seem time-intensive, you end up saving time as your agent works with multiple companies on your behalf to do the "leg work" of shopping for you.

- You get personalized coverages for all your needs either with one company or pieced together with multiple companies, while the broker is managing the different pieces of your program, so you only have one point of contact.

Cons:

- The quote turnaround time is longer. Since there are multiple companies to shop, it can take a little longer to get final pricing and recommendations.

- Every agency sets its own standards, from minimum coverages for the agency to how it handles renewals, claims services, etc., so it is important to understand what the "table stakes" are for the brokerage firm you decide to work with.

- Sometime choice isn't always a good thing, and there are brokers that sell on price and don't understand the different coverage offerings for the companies they represent. So, while the broker can offer the right coverage, instead, they offer you the cheapest cost option, assuming that is what will get the sale done.

4. **Captive Insurance:** This is a form of self-insuring and is becoming popular in the high-net-worth personal insurance market as these individuals' lives become more complex and the standard markets continue to limit their options. This type of coverage is heavily regulated with compliance requirements for how they set up the insurance company. Typically, a third party needs to be hired from the start to make sure everything is thought through from the type of business that will own the insurance company to where the captive company will be domiciled and who will be the administrator and account custodian.

Pros:
- They have the ability to insure assets that may otherwise be uninsurable in the market.

- You retain control of your premium payment. With this model, premium dollars sit in the business account.

- This can potentially help with taxes in two ways if set up properly:

    – Premiums could be seen as deductible expenses.

    – You can make tax-efficient withdrawals.

Cons:

- The setup and administration are complex, and it is a separate business in itself.

- There is a large risk in the beginning based on the exposure(s) compared to/in light of premium dollars collected.

- These types of companies are not always accepted or recognized by major lenders when they need proof of insurance on an asset with a loan.

CONCLUSION

Consumers talk a lot about their balance sheet from an investment and money management perspective. They rarely think about protecting it or losing it all to a home or auto claim. But what happens when you hit a literal bump in the road? Maybe it was a rainy day and you caused a five-car pileup on your way home from a long day at work. How would you pay for that if your insurance wasn't enough? It won't matter if you saved 20% on your coverage if you are writing six-figure checks, being forced to liquidate investments, or, worse, getting your paycheck garnished to cover damages that could have been covered by insurance for pennies on the dollar.

The right insurance program can give you the peace of mind to enjoy life on your terms and the comfort of knowing that if a worse-case situation does occur, you've put the right safeguards in place with the right team to navigate the situation and continue to live life.